What Others Are Saying

"Cal knows that God can! From personal experience and pastoral observations, God's mighty hands and loving arms have carried Cal and others through the dark valleys of life. Nothing is too hard for God. We know this to be true but we sometimes need reminders. Through the local church, Pastor Cal has shepherded his people with a godly passion and vision to trust God. Believers have awakened to the power and grace of Christ, the One who can do the impossible. Yes, He can!"

Emerson Eggerichs
Author of *Love & Respect*

"I have spoken at Northwoods Community Church in Peoria, Illinois, and experienced firsthand the power of the Holy Spirit in action in Pastor Cal's congregation. The amazing stories in *God Can!* stand as proof that the promises of the Bible are as true today as they were in the days of Jesus, Paul, and Peter. If you are looking for motivation and encouragement in your life, then open the front cover and start reading!"

Bruce Wilkinson
Author of *The Prayer of Jabez*

"I believe that everyone has a story to tell. My good friend, Cal Rychener, has woven together a beautiful tapestry of stories from the folks he leads at Northwoods Community Church. These stories speak to the truly transforming power of Jesus Christ on the lives of everyday people like you and me. These types of stories are happening a lot at Northwoods. God is at work. If you like stories that speak to that promise, you're gonna love this book."

Bill Butterworth
Author & Speaker

"Cal Rychener is a leader who jumps into the deep end with both feet. It has been my pleasure to get to know Cal and watch his intense passion for connecting the reality of God with the needs of people. Cal seems to have a clear and piercing vision that the church, both local and global, is God's intended plan for unleashing His presence on the earth and changing lives, and Cal clearly intends to do his part. He is a man who is called and committed to transformation both personally and corporately. I would fully expect lives to be changed under his vision and leadership."

Bob Hamp, Executive Pastor
Pastoral Care Ministries
Gateway Church, Dallas, TX

"America has a lot of great churches and Northwoods Community Church, pastored by Cal Rychener, is certainly one of them. Seeing the life transformation that's happening in Peoria is a terrific reminder that 'God Can!'"

Pat Williams
Orlando Magic senior vice president
Author of *Extreme Focus*

"Pastor Cal and Northwoods Community Church are truly a good witness to the power of God's grace to do the impossible. He listened to our idea of getting his people personally involved in the lives of the people of Jericho by bringing groups for a tour. Here they interact with the people of Jericho, proving to them that Americans don't hate them as they are taught. He understood that in order to change the lives of these people and plant hope, one must give of himself in a very personal way. Not only through giving to the work, but witnessing the work and becoming a part of the community as God did when He sent His only Son to show us the way home. Pastor Cal and his passion for seeing, not only his church, but also others understand God's true redemptive purpose is an example to me. He has become a good friend and encourages me with his words. More importantly, I am an Arab believer and former Muslim, and Pastor Cal has shown me the love of Jesus in my need."

Tass Saada
Author of *Once an Arafat Man*

AMAZING STORIES
OF TRANSFORMED HEARTS
FROM AMERICA'S HEARTLAND

WHEN ALL OF LIFE SEEMS TO SHOUT "YOU CAN'T",

God Can!

Calvin Rychener

WITH AMY PFANSCHMIDT
AND DAVID PFANSCHMIDT

AMAZING STORIES
OF TRANSFORMED HEARTS
FROM AMERICA'S HEARTLAND

WHEN ALL OF LIFE SEEMS TO SHOUT "YOU CAN'T",

God Can!

Calvin Rychener

WITH AMY PFANSCHMIDT
AND DAVID PFANSCHMIDT

INSPIRE
PUBLISHING

PEORIA

Published in Peoria, Illinois, by Inspire Publishing. This, and other Inspire Publishing titles, may be purchased in bulk for educational, business, fund-raising, or sales promotional use. For additional information, please e-mail: dpfanschmidt@sbcglobal.net.

Cover Design: Kirt Manuel
Page Design: Helena Kowal, Diane McBroom, and Brian Trunk

Rychener, Calvin
    God Can!: amazing stories of transformed hearts from America's heartland / Calvin Rychener.

ISBN 978-0-9740491-1-3 (pbk.)

1.   Trust in God - Christianity. 2. Consolation. 3. Disappointment - Religious aspects - Christianity. 4. Suffering - Religious aspects - Christianity.

Printed in the United States of America

To the congregation of Northwoods Community Church:

What an amazing story God is writing through your lives.
What an amazing privilege to be called your pastor.
2 Corinthians 3:3

Contents

Acknowledgments

As this book was taking shape, it became clear to me that writing a book, like leading a church (or even living a life), is a collaborative effort between like-minded people who share a common vision, in this case a vision of declaring to others what God can do. I owe so much to so many for the "story book" you hold in your hands.

To Dawn Henderson, Doug Siefken, Julie Walker, Rick Jeremiah, Alan & Lisa Heth, Vicky Johnson, Mark & Amy Vonachen, Glen & Shelly Penning, and Scott Cramer, thank you for your willingness and courage to share your stories. You are each an inspiring example of what God can do through a life that is fully devoted to Him.

To Amy Pfanschmidt and Dave Pfanschmidt, thank you for your enormous investment in capturing these stories and bringing them to life through the printed page. These stories would not have been told without your dedicated efforts to help share with others what God can do through lives that are fully devoted to Him.

To the incredible staff, elders, and board members of Northwoods Community Church, thanks for your partnership in this ministry and for your insatiable hunger for more of God and what He can do.

May God release thousands more stories of transformed lives through your prayers, faith and obedience.

To my wonderful wife, Susan, thanks for thirty amazing years of living out our story together. Next to God's grace, you're the best thing that ever happened to me. Your devotion to me and belief in me has inspired and encouraged me time and time again to keep on sharing God's story.

To my four children and two (new) in-laws, Kathryn & Andy, Jonathon & Michaela, Victoria and Nathan, no dad could be more thankful or proud of his family than I am of you. You are young and your stories are just getting started, but know that God has great things in store for you as you follow Him. Believe Him for big things!

To my sister and my assistant, Ann Litwiller, thanks for all the little things you do for me on a daily basis to help me keep on telling the story.

To Kirt Manuel for creating a cover design that captures the heart of this story: God Can!

To Angie Conrad, Sally Cloyd, Laurie Trotter, Diane Pfanschmidt, Libby Mucciarone, and Melissa Raguet-Scholfield, thanks for your red ink and excellent input which has helped us better tell these stories.

Dave is especially grateful to his daughter Amy and Pastor Cal for their insistence that he pursue the claims of Christ, and to his wife (Diane) and children (Amy, Brian, Kristin, and Lindsay) for their ongoing love and grace.

Amy wishes to thank her husband, Ben Meyaard, and her children (Bryn, Shay, and Liam) for allowing her the time and freedom to pursue a dream.

To you the reader, thank you for your interest in reading these stories. As you read, I pray your heart will be encouraged and excited by the story that God wants to tell through your own life as you trust and follow Him.

To my Lord Jesus Christ, thanks for Your sacrificial love. Apart from Your amazing grace, none of us would have a story to tell.

Foreword

You will soon meet, and come to know, a dozen of my favorite people. They are joined together on these pages through their love of the Lord Jesus and their Midwestern church. After spending hours interviewing, questioning, understanding, and, in some cases, weeping with the subjects, I have come to know them and their struggles rather well.

They represent varied backgrounds, family heritages, and educational training, but share tremendous inner strength and resolve. It was with much agony and wringing of hands that these stories were birthed. For each of them, the pain was visible and real.

You will meet three couples who have battled - and conquered - their demons. Two couples had to dangle over the edge of the precipice of their extinction before pulling back. They now model - and, in one case, teach - the concept of love and respect. The other couple was forced to face every parent's worst nightmare. United in love, they have weathered a horrid tragedy and lived the very essence of grace.

Six other individuals have tackled a variety of issues. Some had to overcome the horrors of abandonment, alcoholism, attempted suicide, and self-doubt. Others have witnessed transformation in their lives through physical healing, financial re-birth, and spiritual renewal. All are astounded at the extent of the life change they have witnessed. Each was hoping for improvement, but unexpectedly ended up with a major overhaul in nearly every facet of their life.

Just as Jesus used "parables" to do some of His most profound teaching, I hope that the "stories" of these dozen lives will touch your heart and mind. Reading these real stories of real people dealing with real life issues will hopefully affirm once more that God can do any thing, any place, at any time.

What I love the most about these stories is the common thread that not only does God answer these people's prayers, but He also gives them much more than they ever dreamed for themselves.

One "story" is of a woman who wanted the courage to sing in public. But her triumph didn't end with courage. She also got a career, lots of great performance opportunities, and two award-winning CDs.

One couple wanted to save their own marriage. You'll learn how their marriage was healed *and* how they ended up mentoring countless other couples from the brink of separation.

Then there is the story of a couple who were obedient when God called them to a new church *and* ended up free of debt with a beautiful adopted daughter and a new career path.

In her book *Bittersweet*, author Shauna Niequist says, "There are two myths that we tend to believe about our stories; the first is that they're about us, and the second is that because they're about us, they don't matter. But they're not only about us, and they matter more than ever right now. When we, any of us who have been transformed by Christ, tell our own stories, we're telling the story of who God is...

"The big story really is actually being told through our little stories, and by sharing our lives, not just our sermons, we're telling God's story in as reverent and divine ways as it has ever been told."

You may wonder why these people would allow their lives, their struggles, and their inner turmoil to be exposed for all to see. The answer is a simple one: they want to let the world know the difference that Jesus Christ can make in a life.

During my interviews, the most frequently heard mantra was: "If my story can help even one person overcome similar pain, then it's all worth it." My hope, and theirs, is that you may be that person.

Dave Pfanschmidt
September 6, 2011

Re-Awakening

I still remember, like it was yesterday, the "God moment" that occurred in my life over 23 years ago. I was a 29-year-old pastor, three years into my first pastorate, having arrived at my first church as the new Senior Pastor following my graduation from seminary in June of 1986. Things were going well at the 150-member church in Grabill, Indiana, a quaint little town in the northeastern part of the state. We were growing, I loved the members of our church and community, new people were attending the church, and numerous new believers had recently committed their lives to Jesus Christ.

Yet, for all the positive indications that God was indeed at work in our church, something was stirring in my heart that I could not escape. I referred to it then as a "pastoral depression" of sorts; today I understand that it was the process of vision formation through which God will often take a leader on his way from what **is** to what **can be**. However, since I was a young pastor at that point and didn't understand the process, I really feared that I might battle feelings of dissatisfaction and depression the rest of my life. Boy, was I wrong!

In late March of 1988, my wife and I were returning from 12 days of rest and relaxation in the warm sunshine of Sarasota, Florida. Driving up Interstate 75 that day, I had no idea that the program I was listening to on the radio that morning was about to rock my world and change the course of my ministry. The program happened to be an interview with Bill Hybels, the dynamic young pastor of a mega-church phenomenon in South Barrington, Illinois, known as Willow Creek.

Bill shared his heart that day about how God had called him to build a church that would intentionally reach out to people who were far from God, rather than simply serving those who were already followers of Christ. As he spoke about how the good news of Jesus Christ had radically transformed the lives of thousands of people since Willow Creek's inception in 1975, I was gripped by a strange sense that this was exactly the kind of ministry for which I had been made.

Tears were streaming down my face as I listened, and I remember uttering a simple prayer from the bottom of my heart that day: "God, what Bill is describing right now resonates with everything in my heart. If there is any way I could ever be a part of a church like that, please open the door for me."

It was a defining moment in my young ministry life.

I had no idea where my prayer would lead me, nor did I have a sense that I was to do anything other than wait on God to make clear what my next steps should be. All I knew for certain was that God had used the radio interview with Bill to breathe fresh vision and clarity into my heart.

I was also beginning to understand why I was dissatisfied and depressed. I had been suppressing a huge part of who God had made me to be and how He had wired me up for ministry. I also knew that it was probably going to mean a big change for me, since the kind of ministry I envisioned was not likely to be a good fit with the church I was currently pastoring. So I continued to work hard and wait.

After hearing that interview, I understood that, as a pastor with an evangelistic bent, I needed to be a part of a ministry that was intentional and strategic about reaching people far from God.

Fast forward to late January of 1990. I had been called to attend a meeting with a couple of our denominational leaders at which time they informed me of a new church plant that was slated to launch in Peoria, Illinois, on March 25, 1990. Seven months of hard work had already been invested in laying the foundation for this new church. A core group of leaders and volunteers had been established. Some 32,000 phone calls had been made to residents throughout the Peoria area and 2,500 interested people had received invitations to the first service. Things were ready to roll. "However", they said, "we have a couple of problems."

"What kind of problems?" I asked.

Their answer: "We don't have a pastor and we don't have a place to meet."

I was like, "Wow, you do have some problems! So, why are you sharing them with me?"

They responded, "We believe you are the answer to the biggest problem. We would like you to consider becoming the pastor of this new church plant."

Even before they had finished asking me, something within me stirred and took me back to that defining moment in the car almost two years earlier. The Spirit of God whispered to my heart, "Cal, this is what that moment was about." In my heart, I knew before I left their office that day that I was going to be moving in very short order. I also knew that my next step was to make the five-hour drive to Peoria to meet with the core team.

But over the next few days, as my wife and I began to discuss the possibility of a move, a whole host of obstacles and objections bombarded our minds.

Wow, if we do this, we hardly have any time to wrap up our ministry in Grabill since the new church in Peoria is only a few weeks away from launching. Would it really be wise to just up and move that quickly? Moreover, I have never planted a church before and know nothing about how to launch a new church. Beyond that, I really don't know anything at all about how to build a church to reach spiritual seekers. I know only a few people on the launch team, and I know next to nothing about the city of Peoria.

You can tell I wasn't exactly dripping with faith and confidence.

Besides all of these objections, Susan and I were only months removed from one of the most excruciating experiences of our lives. We had just buried our newborn son, Christopher, only 10 hours after his birth on November 11, 1989. We were crushed and still raw with the pain and disappointment of that loss. So nothing about this move, particularly in this season of our lives, made sense.

However, I have discovered in over 40 years of walking with God that one whisper from His Spirit can trump all objections. I knew God was laying this opportunity at my feet. In spite of all of my human objections and apparent disqualifications, the Spirit of God kept downloading words of confidence and faith to my heart and reminding me that the God I serve can do the impossible through weak and imperfect human beings who trust Him and obey His promptings!

When the powers of darkness and circumstances and human reasoning marshal their evidence against you to tell you, "You can't," just remind them that "God can!"

Thus, on March 25, 1990, I had the privilege of welcoming 332 people to our first service in a renovated bowling alley known as the Christian Center, and Northwoods Community Church was born. Over the intervening 21 years, we have grown to a church of nearly 4,000 people. But far more significant to me than the number of people who attend each week, are the thousands of lives that have been transformed by the power of Jesus Christ.

There are literally thousands of people who have come through the doors of Northwoods at one time or another over the past 21 years, who could tell you that whatever human impossibility you may be facing in your life today, whenever life screams at you, "It can't be done; it can't happen, your life or situation can't change," the last word remains, "God can... and does... do the impossible!"

In the following pages, you are going to read real stories of real people who have discovered that "God can." He can take difficult situations and transform them by His power. He can infuse hope into hopeless situations. He can awaken fresh dreams and use us in ways we never dreamed. He can heal broken bodies and damaged emotions. He can restore fractured marriages. He can set us free from the past and bring us into a new day. He can do the impossible!

I pray that as you read these stories, you will find hope for your situation and will find yourself stepping out to embrace what God can and will do for you.

Before you begin, I feel that I need to share a personal concern with you about a particular issue that I simply wouldn't want to become a stumbling block for anyone who reads this book.

All of the stories contained in this book come from precious people whose lives have been changed at Northwoods Community Church and whom I've had the privilege of pastoring and leading.

While I thank God for this immense privilege, I am sensitive to the fact that in telling these stories, my name gets used more often than I am comfortable with, and at other times it may appear as if we are exalting Northwoods as some kind of "super-church." Nothing could be further from our intent. Our only intent is to glorify the name of our Lord Jesus Christ, who can do amazing things in any life and any church where He is welcomed, worshiped and loved.

At the end of the day, none of us will mind if you forget our names, if only this book will have helped you to trust the God who can do amazing things in your life.

These stories are powerful testimonies of what God has done. That word "testimony" contains within it the concept of a seed that is sown in the heart of the one who hears it. As you read this book, you may find your life experience overlapping with a particular testimony that awakens a hunger in your heart. You may find yourself saying, "Lord, will you do that for me?" That is the purpose of testimony — to give you hope that what God has done for one, He will do for you.

So friend, **whatever impossibility you are facing today that you think can't be solved, I have good news for you: *God can*!**

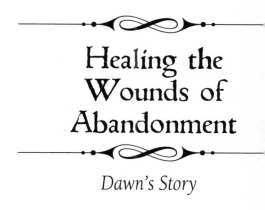

Healing the Wounds of Abandonment

Dawn's Story

> *"But then I will win her back once again.*
> *I will lead her into the desert*
> *and speak tenderly to her there."*
>
> HOSEA 2:14

In his book, *Think Differently, Live Differently,* author Bob Hamp shares the story of a couple who were members of a traveling acrobatic troupe during the frontier days of America. Sadly, while on the road to a performance, their baby boy tumbled from their wagon in the middle of a remote wilderness. In their panicked attempts to find him, they backtracked their wagon route for days, but all to no avail. Their little boy was gone.

Meanwhile, a farmer and his wife, passing by that way one day, heard the cries of a small baby. Parting the grass beside the trail, they were startled to discover a baby boy lying in a ditch by the road. Though the story is too long to recount in detail here, the bottom line is that for the next 15 – 20 years of that boy's life, a tug-of-war ensued between two seemingly contradictory sides of his psyche.

His external desires were to be seen as the responsible, well-behaved, non-risk-taking, aspiring farmer that his adoptive father and mother had raised him to be. But his internal desire, which he could never explain, was to climb, jump, and be an acrobat.

Unplugged from the knowledge of who his true parents were and who he truly was designed to be, the boy spent his life trying to deny and suppress the inner voices and urges that suggested he was made for something more. Eventually he conformed to what those around him wanted him to be.

If this sounds like a familiar story, it is because to some extent, it is each of our stories. The truth is simply that all of us were born into this world separated from the One Person, our Heavenly Father, who alone has the blueprint for who we were designed to be. Devoid of connection with Him and His input into our unique DNA, we can spend a lifetime searching for that illusive sense of meaning, fulfillment, and belonging – always searching but never finding.

At our root, we have all suffered a wound of abandonment – not because our Heavenly Father abandoned us, but because we have fallen off the wagon and are no longer in touch with our true identity. That primal wound can be made better or worse depending on the loving care, or lack thereof, that we may have received from our earthly families. But even in the best of families, it remains for us to find our way back to a relationship with the Heavenly Father, who alone can heal our wounds and set us free to be who we were designed to be.

Dawn Henderson is one young lady who, in spite of her wounds, found her way home to the Heavenly Father and is living the vibrant, exciting life of a "Creative Arts acrobat" in our church today. As you read her story, I pray you will sense faith rising up in your heart to believe that God can... heal your wounds of abandonment.

Even in her earliest memories, the sense of abandonment is always there.

Dawn Henderson's biological father left her mother when she was very young. Her parents divorced when she was just two years old, and Dawn's mother was left to raise four daughters, of whom Dawn was the youngest. Her father was in and out of their lives after that. Although he did have some visitation rights, Dawn's father eventually remarried and moved to Tennessee with his new wife. Occasionally the girls would visit during the summer, but for the most part, they stayed with their mother in Washington, Illinois, and time with their father was rare.

When Dawn was seven years old, her mother also remarried. One year later, her mother had a baby boy and completed their family. Dawn says of the remarriage, "I got a wonderful father. He became the man I considered my daddy."

As a child, Dawn did not attend church regularly. She says, "Our family was essentially unchurched. We would occasionally go to a Catholic mass on Easter or Christmas Eve. I remember it because we would get all dressed up, but it didn't mean anything to us. I'm guessing we went to Catholic mass because my mom's parents had done the same thing and it's what she knew.

"Despite that, my mom instilled in all her daughters very Biblical principles. We didn't pray together or go to church. We just knew that my parents believed there was a God. My mother taught us about forgiveness, about unconditional love, about loyalty, and about honesty."

Growing up as the youngest daughter in a family of mostly girls, perhaps it should come as no surprise that Dawn loved to dance and perform. She developed these talents throughout her teenage years. Then, Dawn found what she was certain was love.

She remembers, "Right out of high school, I met a guy. I ended up dropping out of college to get married. We were both professional dancers. It all happened pretty fast, when I was in my early 20s. We had lots of job offers from everywhere in the United States... Vegas, Broadway, Branson... pretty much anywhere we wanted to go."

Because of family ties, Dawn and her husband kept the Peoria area as their home base. They gave private lessons locally and also travelled on the couples' dancing circuit. Their lives seemed very full. Then, God began knocking on Dawn's heart.

Dawn says, "A friend we had met, and who had taken a dance class from us, attended a small church in central Illinois. My husband and I both thought he was a great guy, so when he invited us to go to church with him, it was hard to say 'no.' I'll admit that I was completely opposed. My attitude was 'Why would we go to church? We've never gone to church.'

"For whatever reason, my husband really wanted to go. As I observed the service, it seemed to me that there was a lot of craziness going on. I was convinced those people belonged in the loony bin! Everything was just completely foreign to anything I had ever seen. The whole experience felt funny to me.

"At the end of the service, the pastor said, 'I feel like God gave me a word for someone,' and then he asked me to stand up.

"I'm thinking, 'Get me out of here!'

"He prophesied over me and talked about me being abandoned as a child and that something significant had happened in my life when I was seven years old that had set me on a new course. That was, of course, when my mother had remarried.

"We left after the service and I told our friend in the parking lot, 'What were you thinking? That was crazy!' But inside, I realized that prophetic words had been spoken over me that could not be disputed. I may have felt uncomfortable and out of my element, but the things the pastor said to me were totally true. I was reeling from that whole experience and vowed never to go there again.

"About a week later, we had dinner with the same friend who had invited us to the small church, and he apologized. He said, 'I don't know what I was thinking. I suddenly saw it through your eyes and went "Ooops."'

"But he also said that he heard there was a church on the north side of Peoria called 'Northwoods' that he felt we should check out. I was hesitant, but he convinced us it was totally different than our first church experience.

"We attended a service not long after that, and it happened to be Easter Sunday. There was a big dance production as part of the service, and since that was our thing, it seemed a whole lot more normal. I was blown away that they would even have dancing in a church. It was very well done, and it just felt like me. I felt like they were trying to speak my language. I got what they were doing. As a total outsider, it felt like they really had it all together.

"About two months later, a different friend invited us to another service [at Northwoods]. During that two-month period, something inside me felt like change was coming. I couldn't put my finger on it, but I sensed something was stirring in me."

———••◦∞◦••———

Shortly thereafter, in early June of 1999, Dawn and her husband were offered positions doing choreography and dance at a theatre in Branson, Missouri.

"At the time," says Dawn, "I thought this move must have been what I had sensed was coming. We made the decision at that time to go full professional and not teach anymore. All that timing seemed to line up just right.

"But at the same time, another friend invited us to attend Northwoods with her. We actually attended for six weeks straight before moving to Branson. Even though this was 10 years ago, I can remember it like it was yesterday. Every word and every song felt like they were just for me. I felt like someone was coming after me. It almost made me mad that every message seemed as if it was written specifically for me. Every weekend experience was so personal."

Two weeks before leaving for Branson, Dawn took a "Yes" packet at the end of the service. Taking a packet indicates making a decision to follow Christ, and the packet itself is full of helpful resources to assist the new believer on the next steps of his or her spiritual journey.

Dawn says, "It was scary because I really wasn't sure all that I was saying 'yes' to. I was confused and afraid. I didn't want my husband or my family to know, so I hid the 'Yes' packet in my purse. I was really freaked about it because I was so scared. I thought everyone would think I was crazy. I felt like I couldn't explain why I had done it or how my life felt different now.

"I remember one week before we left, being in the service and just sobbing. I was overwhelmed with all that was going on in my life between the impending move and all the God stuff happening at the same time. Judy Sinn, a Northwoods' member who was a complete stranger at the time, came up to me and invited me to her home.

"She said, 'I just want to pray for you and help you if you have any questions on your journey.'

"I went to her house and we sat on the back deck. The first thing she said to me was, 'There are no dumb questions.' I felt like she knew what I was struggling with. She was so amazing and so loving and so eager to give me a safe place to explore the claims of Christ."

Coming from this loving, supportive environment, what happened next came as even more of a shock to Dawn.

"Life got really difficult after that. After we had been in Branson for three weeks, my husband did an about-face. He told me that he was struggling with things in his life and was considering divorce. I was in shock. I really thought we had a fairy-tale marriage. We were healthy and happy, and then he shared with me that he felt as if he was living a lie and that this was never what he wanted. It was very hard stuff.

"I remember, during those next few months, thinking that perhaps I had made a wrong decision trusting in God. My logic was something like, 'If God is good, then this wouldn't be happening to me.' So I went through a season, the first six or seven months we were in Branson, of trying to sort out in my mind who I really was and what I was after in my life.

"Tentatively and cautiously, I stepped into having a conversation with God. I was afraid to talk to Him because I felt like He was disappointed in me and I didn't know why. I felt like, 'I'm a good girl, God. I didn't do anything wrong.'

"I just had lots of fear that a pattern was forming in my life of abandonment. I felt like my dad didn't want me and left, and now my husband didn't want me and was going to leave. From this I drew the conclusion that God didn't want me either, and eventually He too would abandon me.

"My husband and I stuck it out about a year. I am an avid reader and started pouring myself into Scripture during that time. I remember my husband coming home at night from rehearsals and I would be in the middle of the bed with the Bible open, reading Scripture. The first thing out of his mouth would be, 'Are you reading that damned book again?' The force of his words coming at me just stole my breath and made me feel like I didn't even know him. My reaction was to hide the Bible rather than stand up to him."

On the first weekend of June in 2000, Dawn and her husband drove back to Illinois for a friend's wedding. The next morning, Dawn's husband got into their car and drove away, leaving her with literally nothing but what she had brought for the weekend visit. They had been married for just over seven years. She has only spoken to him once since.

"I was numb," she says. "Every day I felt like I couldn't catch my breath.

"I stayed in Illinois with my sister for three weeks, and then she and her husband drove me to where my parents live, which is just outside of Springfield, Missouri. My dad took me in his truck over to our condo in Branson. I'll never forget putting the key in the lock, opening the door, and finding the condo completely empty.

"It was stark. I remember just standing there and hanging my head, and my dad saying, 'Come on, honey. Let me take you home.'

"I told my parents that I didn't know what was next for me. I was in complete shock. I told them, 'I don't know where to go from here. I feel lost.'

"My mom said to me, 'Everything you need is in you, and you just need to tap into it. Take the time you need to figure it out.'

"I stayed with my parents from July until November. What happened in those months was significant. It was a turning point for me. I got a part-time job working in a women's clothing store just to make some money. I was saving money so that I could buy a car at an auction and try to figure out what was next for me.

"When I finally got a car, I would spend hours driving the hills of Missouri, crying and talking to God and trying to figure out who I was. I asked God to show Himself to me and told Him that I needed to know that He was real. I needed to know that I mattered. I needed to know that He had a plan for me."

————··◁∞▷··————

"Ten years later, I long for what I had in those four months. I was in the worst hell I could ever imagine, but my relationship with God during that time was incredible. I could sense the nearness of His presence during those four months. I couldn't get away from Him. He was on me with this warm blanket of grace as I cried and cried and cried. I kept asking God over and over, 'Where do I go now? What is next for me?'"

In the fall of that year, God answered in an unexpected way. One of Dawn's old friends, who now lived in Boston, got in touch with her. "She had heard that my husband and I had separated, and she wanted me to come out for a visit. She invited me to stay with her for two weeks and even sent me a plane ticket. I went out East in early November. When I got off the plane, Ann met me at baggage claim, handed me the keys to her apartment and said, 'You're not going to believe what's happened. I have to go to the West Coast for work, but I want you to stay at my apartment.'"

At her friend's urging, Dawn spent the next two weeks in Boston. Her friend had even planned two weekend getaways for her, the first of which included a trip to New York and the closing show of *Saigon* on Broadway. It was the second weekend of her trip, however, that provided the answers for which Dawn had been praying.

Dawn remembers, "The last weekend I went to the Cape. Being November, it was deserted and really cold and stormy the whole weekend. I don't think it ever stopped raining the whole time I was there. Each day I would get up, walk the beach in the rain, and just sob.

"My big request to God was, 'I need to hear from You where I should go now.' I felt like I wanted to go back to Peoria. My sisters were all there, and I knew that I needed to build a life for myself and needed their support to do it. But I felt ashamed to go home. I felt torn.

"Each morning I would walk the beach and talk with God. I just felt so very alone.

"On my last day, I was walking the beach in the rain, and I looked up to see this big black dog running full force toward me. I felt no fear. Far behind the dog came this little figure. I didn't know if it was a man or a woman. As the figure got closer, I realized it was a very, very old woman.

"The dog was hopping all around me in the pouring rain, and the woman stopped and apologized for letting the dog off his leash. She said, 'I am so sorry if the dog scared you. I didn't think anyone else would be on the beach today.' I told her it was fine and we each went on our way.

"There were these big boulders jutting out into the water. Every day I had been climbing on them and just sitting out in the ocean, talking with God. I did so again, and a little while later, the woman and her dog came back from their walk. The dog swam out to me in the water. I came back onto the beach so the dog would come back in to its owner.

"When my feet hit the sand, the little old lady was right there in front of me. She saw that I was crying, and she reached out both her hands and put them on my cheeks. She said to me, 'You need to go home. That's what is next for you. . . home.' I knew in that moment that I was moving back to Peoria.

"I stood there in silence amidst my tears, and she said, 'You are His favorite. He loves you. God loves you, and He does have a plan. Trust Him. Go home and trust Him.'

"It was a crazy experience. I felt in that moment like I was looking into the eyes of God.

"Standing there in the pouring rain, the little old lady unfolded her story. She told me she was a nun staying in a cottage down the beach with five other nuns, the oldest of whom had terminal cancer. She said that when she got up that morning, God spoke to her and told her that He had a message for someone she would encounter on the beach.

"At Northwoods, Cal has taught so many times about how when it is God's way, He opens up every door and removes every obstacle. That is so true! When I flew back to Springfield, Missouri, the next day, my mom told me the district manager of the store where I was working had called and wanted to meet with me right away.

"When I went into work the next day, my manager took me to the back room and said, 'We're opening a new store in a little town up north in Illinois called Bloomington. We would like you to be the store's manager. The only problem is you have to be there in a week.'" (Bloomington is less than an hour from Peoria)

Dawn says, "I was stunned. Here God had even provided a way for me to get home. "I drove home the day before Thanksgiving. I rented a little one-room house for $220 a month. In that tiny shack of a house, I had so many amazing encounters with Jesus. He met me there. I was hungry for Scripture and hungry to be the woman He wanted me to become."

---···❀···---

As Easter of 2001 approached, Dawn received a call from Kirk Moser, the production director at Northwoods. Dawn remembers, "He had heard I was back in town and wanted to know if I would dance and do some choreography for the Easter service.

"I said, 'Absolutely not! I'm not ready. I don't know if I'll ever dance again. It's just too soon.'

"Being who he is, Kirk said, 'I understand, but just listen to the music and see what you think.' He sent me the music and I ended up dancing at Northwoods for Easter in 2001. It was a great experience, and I felt like I needed to be there, so I started attending regularly.

"In June, the Creative Arts director called and said he wanted to meet with me. We got to know each other over lunch, and he asked if I would apply for the Creative Arts administrative assistant position.

"Meanwhile, I wanted to proceed with the divorce, but I had no money. That summer, I got online and printed all the paperwork I thought I needed. Then I called the courthouse and asked if I could have an appointment with a judge.

"They gave me the appointment I had requested, and when I showed up, it was just me, the judge, and a court reporter. He asked me why I didn't have an attorney, so I shared a bit of what had happened. In the papers I had filled out, I listed 'irreconcilable differences' as the reason for my divorce request. The judge explained that in the state of Illinois, a counseling period of six months is required for that cause before a divorce decree can be issued.

"Then he said, 'I feel like there is more that you are not telling me. I need to know more.'

"Then the judge leaned over and said, 'Did he abandon you?' At that point, I just started crying. The judge marked through 'irreconcilable differences,' wrote 'abandonment', signed the divorce papers, and told me it was done."

In September of 2001, Dawn got the job at Northwoods and began work. The close-knit community provided her with a place to heal. She says, "I was able to be who I really was and still be accepted and loved."

Three years later, the Creative Arts director left and Dawn was promoted into his position. At this point, Dawn says, "It all started to make sense. It's like God had been preparing me for where I am today. I know that I wouldn't have been prepared for my current job without all the experiences I had earlier in my life."

And those experiences from earlier in life, particularly those of abandonment, were still wounds that had not been fully healed. Even with everything going well on the professional front, Dawn remained vulnerable emotionally, and her next loss hit her hard.

She says, "In 2005, the dad who raised me died suddenly. The loss devastated my sisters and brother. It was a very difficult time. I think we girls had an extra strong tie to him because we knew that he chose us. It takes a special kind of man to take on a wife and four little girls.

"In my case, it brought back all of the abandonment issues one more time. I had always been Daddy's little girl, and it felt like another man I loved had left me. I was really hurting."

About a year later, Dawn had the opportunity to attend a conference focused on healing. The closer the conference got, the more that her subconscious tugged the painful memories of abandonment to the forefront.

She remembers, "For the six months leading up to the conference, I had a recurring dream. It wasn't an every night dream, but it would pop up every week or so.

"In my dream, I was a little girl. I wasn't sure how old, but I knew I was little. I kept feeling like I was looking out a window. From this window I could see a yard and a driveway and a chain link fence across the street. In the dream, I always felt very, very sad. When I would wake up, I would think, 'What the heck was that all about?'

"Right before the healing conference, my mom was in Peoria for a visit and I told her about this weird dream that I kept having. All of a sudden, she started crying and asking me to forgive her. She shared with me that the dream was from when I was two years old and my dad left.

"She told me that I would go downstairs and sit in the foyer, looking out the window, waiting for my dad to come home. She said, 'I was so devastated that I couldn't get out of bed. I slept most of the day. I remember coming out of the bedroom and seeing you down there on the landing, watching out the window.'

"By that point in my life, I had been through my own adult devastation and understood what she had experienced. I said, 'Mom, you don't owe me an apology. I well remember what it feels like not to be able to breathe. You raised me well and you loved me, and I'm okay.'"

After talking to her mother about the dream, Dawn felt that she was in a very good place emotionally. She says, "Following that visit from my mom, I went to the healing conference. One aspect of this particular conference was signing up for some healing prayer time with their team. I was feeling really apprehensive about going because everything in my life was so good. I was in a really sweet spot with Jesus and feeling in good communion with Him and very much covered in His love.

"Things at home were good. Things at church were good. My life was just in a really good place. I remember thinking, 'What am I going to talk to the prayer team about? Maybe they'll let me pray for them!'

"I remember sitting in the little chapel with the three people on the team who were going to pray for me. When I told them things were great in my life and that maybe I should pray for them, they smiled and suggested that maybe we should pray and ask God if there was something He wanted to talk about with me.

"After we had started to pray, one of the ladies on the team looked up and said, 'Why don't you tell me about your dream?' Since I hadn't said a word about my dream to anyone other than my mom, I was stunned and started to weep.

"I shared with them what happened in my dream and then what happened with my mom. The woman on the prayer team said she didn't think that was all of it and that we needed to ask God for more wisdom about the dream. We prayed and prayed, and I cried and cried.

"She asked me to go back to the place I was when I was two and to describe what I was seeing when I was sitting in front of the window. As I was describing it, she said to me, 'Dawn, I want to know where Jesus was when that happened to you. Where was He?'

"Then it hit me. I had felt my entire life that He was never present until I relented and said I wanted him there. The woman said to me again, 'Dawn, where was He?' I realized in that moment that I was in His lap and He was rocking me.

"I felt like there was this big gaping hole within me that instantly closed up for the first time in my life.

"Something inside me said, 'He would never leave you. He formed you, He wanted you, He never left you... even when you were two years old.'

"Then the woman said, 'There's more and you know it, but you have to tell us.' That made me cry even harder, because I didn't want to tell anybody. I had never shared my feelings about him leaving with anyone.

"The lady on my right suddenly took both my hands and said, 'When God brought your mom and dad together, He knew that He needed another girl, and that girl needed to be you to fulfill His purpose. He picked you. You were chosen by Him. You were formed by Him.'

"For my entire life, I had always wondered if I had been born a boy would my father have stayed. I felt that after three girls, if I had been born a boy, he wouldn't have left us and our family would have been able to stay together.

"For the first time in my life, sitting there with the healing prayer team, I had the feeling that I had the freedom to really be me. I am who God designed me to be. I didn't get that before. I had lived a life thinking somehow it could have all been better. But in that moment, the realization came over me that it wouldn't have been better. In fact, He needed me to be me and to do what I'm doing today."

God has had His hand in Dawn's story all along, from the moment that He created her. And He never ceases to surprise her with all of the ways that He has shown up in her life. One of the happiest surprises of late has been that Dawn and her sisters are growing in their relationship with their biological father. Though humans may abandon her, Dawn knows that God never will.

Of her journey of faith, Dawn says, "I guess I've just learned to say, 'God I'm open. My arms are wide open to You and wherever You want to lead me.'"

Remember our story of the acrobat? That story has an unbelievable ending. Through a strange set of circumstances, an acrobatic troupe came to this young farmer's town. The boy, now a young man, talked his parents into letting him attend the performance, and they even decided to attend with him.

It was there, amid the excitement of the show, that the young man's adoptive mother found herself standing off to the side of the tent with an older female member of the acrobatic troupe. In their discussion, the older woman made mention of how excited this woman's son seemed to be by all the acrobats and their flying feats. Then she mentioned something that would forever change all of their lives. She said, rather sadly, that she had lost her baby years ago when he had fallen out of the wagon probably not far from this town.

The farmer's wife, badly shaken but knowing that it would be wrong to conceal the secret, then revealed to her son's rightful mother the story of how they had found this baby in the ditch one day and that this young man was indeed the long-lost son of this famous acrobatic family. This, in turn, triggered a series of events that saw the son finally realize his long-suppressed dream of becoming a part of the acrobatic troupe and discovering the freedom, for the first time in his life, of becoming who he was designed to be.

It's Dawn's story, and it can be your story too, if you will bring your wounds of abandonment to the Heavenly Father and let Him show you who you were designed to be.

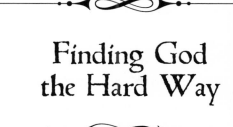

Finding God
the Hard Way

Doug's Story

"Humility, recovering alcoholics like to say, is stark raving honesty.
Recovery from the disease cannot be initiated until
the deadly denial dwelling in the subterranean personality
of the drunk is exposed and acknowledged.

ABBA'S CHILD BY BRENNAN MANNING

There have been times over the past 20 years when I have
forgotten just how much of a miraculous turnaround God has
performed in some people's lives. Were you to meet them today, you
simply wouldn't believe where they were when God got hold of their
lives. One of those guys is a good friend of mine named Doug.

He sits right down front at church every Sunday, center section,
front row. And then, during the time of prayer and worship following
each service, he usually stays behind for 10 minutes or so, head bowed,

eyes closed, just drinking in the Lord's presence. Often I just smile and shake my head at the wonder of the transformation in Doug's life.

If I remember correctly, I met Doug at the gym one day. I don't exactly recall how we first struck up a conversation, but I could tell I liked this guy right from the start and was impressed that he had been a heck of a football player in his day. He even played a year for the Nebraska Cornhuskers. Another thing I noticed about Doug, right from the start, was that he always seemed to be in a relationship with some young lady, just sort of bouncing from one to the next.

I mention this only to say that before Doug came to grips with the emptiness inside him and his need for a relationship with Christ, he would resort to two drugs of choice to numb the pain: women and alcohol. This is why, when I met with him up in the psych ward the day after he had attempted to take his life, I knew we would have to deal with his bondage to both drugs if he was ever going to be free.

And today, he is a walking testimony to the truth of John 8:36, which says, "He whom the Son sets free is free indeed." Doug's story is a reminder that God can set you free from any hurts, habits, and hang-ups in your life.

Doug Siefken possessed a quick wit, an engaging smile, and the gift of gab. From his earliest days, he was surrounded by a great, loving family. He had a high paying job and lots of friends. He was both handsome and athletic. And he was empty.

He says, "From the beginning, I was blessed far beyond what anyone could reasonably expect. I am the product of two young, loving parents whose values were forged by their difficult lives. My mom is German and lost two brothers in the war. Dad was the oldest of three.

At 12 years of age, he was forced into somewhat of a paternal role by the passing of his father

"I was the baby of a family of four, born while my father was still pursuing a business degree from North Dakota State. After college, Dad relocated us to central Illinois having accepted an offer from Caterpillar. He worked his way up the corporate ladder, ultimately becoming president of CEFCU, one of the largest and most innovative credit unions in the world. While strict, I can't remember the old man ever raising his voice.

"Our family attended a Protestant denominational church about twice a month. Nothing about this was fun for an antsy kid. I couldn't wait for the sermon to come to an end. Our church was very staid and structured. I don't think there were many kids who enjoyed the rigidity. The worst part was the confirmation process: two years, twice a week, all memorization. There are no fond memories."

After graduation from Pekin High School, Siefken followed his brother to the University of Nebraska. Doug describes his introduction to fraternity life: "My brother was a year ahead of me in school and a member of a Lutheran fraternity at Nebraska. I went to a rush party with his fraternity out in Estes Park, Colorado. I met four or five other kids they were trying to rush and really liked them. Of course, we got drunker than we should have.

"During high school, I probably only drank two or three times. Pekin had some pretty rough kids at the time and I was not in the group that we called 'hoods'. I was an athlete and got pretty good grades. I had a curfew and never stayed out late. In general, I was a pretty good kid."

Siefken played a year of college football. The Cornhuskers had just won back-to-back (1970–71) national titles. The players were somewhat lionized and the atmosphere was electrifying.

"The fall of '72 is when I learned how to drink," Doug says. "Every game was an excuse to get drunk. After most home games, our fraternity would host what we called 'woodsies.' We would take a date to a bonfire out in the country, drink heavily, and serenade them with lewd songs. We were a classy bunch!

"It was almost a badge of honor to be able to drink all night and get up the next day and share your war stories with your buddies. That mindset defined my persona and that mentality carried on for the rest of my life up until the last three or four years."

Doug now realizes his college days set the tone for the rest of his life. He says, "I can't honestly say that there was ever a week when I did not drink. From the first day when I went to Nebraska until just a few years ago, that was simply my way of life. It was a joke with my friends. We called ourselves 'drunks'. We knew we were drunks, not alcoholics, because alcoholics went to meetings. We were what I would call 'functional alcoholics'. It was simply part of our perceived manhood.

"After a while, it got bad. Back then, I never felt that I was negligent with my kids, although now I realize I was because I didn't raise them with Christ. I got divorced when my son was eight and my daughter was six. I guess you would say we simply fell out of love. There was no cheating, per se, but I was a stockbroker at the time and would go out after work for three or four hours drinking doubles almost every day. In that regard, I was cheating on my wife. It wasn't with another woman, but I wasn't spending time with her, as I should have."

When Siefken's divorce became final, he did everything within his power to see his children as much as possible. He remembers, "I coached every team they were on and convinced the judge to let me see them every day after school. I loved my kids and, regardless of what happened in the marriage, I wanted to be a part of their lives.

"On the weekends when I had my kids I was still drinking. I didn't go out, but I would get a couple of big boy vodkas and mix them with Kool-Aid and just drink at my place."

Religion was not on the Siefken family's radar screen. Doug says, "I would have to say our family was not spending a lot of time in church. We did go to a Methodist church a couple times, but there was no ongoing relationship with Christ.

"If the children sensed that I had a relationship with God, it had to be from copies of *The Upper Room* daily devotionals that I had in the bathroom. I'm sure they saw those and wondered what the deal was but we certainly never discussed anything about religion."

Doug made a good living as a stockbroker, but had no pride in his profession. He says, "For 20 years I toiled in a profession I absolutely abhorred. The things I saw in that industry didn't just shock me, they made me want to come home and take a shower. Yet I always thought I could do it 'the right way'. I couldn't. It was capitalism at its finest. Place people in a position to fleece others and they will. Don't allow yourself to think otherwise.

"I would like to say that was the reason I drank, but I know it wasn't. I drank because I simply liked to drink. It was an escape. If something good happened at work, we drank. If it was a bad day at work, we drank. There was always an excuse.

"I can look back now and see that God had a plan for me. Now I can see that He was working on me and waiting for me to spiral downward until I hit bottom and had no other direction to turn but toward Him.

"Early in 2000, the financial markets crashed. It was a bad time to be a broker and even worse for an alcoholic broker. I became more and more disenchanted with my job, but not quite enough to do anything about it. I would just drink and hope, then drink some more and sink deeper into that abyss. The markets plummeted to levels few imagined.

"It was then I decided to do something about it. I had just come off a weekend bender and was shaking so badly Monday morning that I had a tough time driving to the emergency room. I had abrasions on my forehead from falling face-first into the wall or floor. That was when the pain of continuing became greater than the pain of quitting. It led me to Alcoholics Anonymous.

"At about that point, I started to hunger for a relationship with the church. I know now that God was chasing me. Over the course of three or four years, I had at least 10 to 15 people try and talk to me about Northwoods Community Church. To a person, they were all terrific comments. Everyone talked about what an exceptional church experience it was and how different it was from the normal run-of-the-mill church. So I started to think about going to church again.

"But the best of intentions on a Thursday or Friday can really change by the weekend. After I had been drinking Saturday night, I'd wake up Sunday with a hangover and think, 'They're going to smell the booze on me.'"

As new people started to enter Doug's life, he sensed a nudge from God.

He recalls, "One day I was at the gym and was on a treadmill next to a lady named Mary Rose Mitchell. She was a Northwoods' member and always seemed to have something to say about the Lord or about church. I thought of her as the kind of person where you want to duck across the street so you don't have to meet. You know, a 'Jesus freak.' But she had a captive audience in me on the treadmill. I wasn't going to be rude and go to another machine. She just gently dripped on me to the point where she brought me an audio tape of a Northwoods service and told me she wanted me to listen to it. She even said she was going to quiz me to make sure I had listened. Gradually, because of her nudging perhaps, I developed a hunger for God.

"Meanwhile, I took my two kids to an amusement park over by Cincinnati called Kings Island. While we were there, my kids saw this great T-shirt and on the front it said, 'I only have time for one person a day. Today is not your day and tomorrow doesn't look good either.' The kids liked the shirt and they bought it for me.

"A couple of months later, I was wearing the shirt at the gym and I see this guy walk in sporting a smile. I had seen him a few times before, and each time he had that same 'I love life' smile. We had never been introduced, but Cal Rychener started a conversation with me by saying he liked my shirt.

"We struck up a conversation and he told me what he did. I said I had been kind of thinking about going back to church and explained a little bit of my situation. He invited me to the Christmas production, and even got me four tickets. I went to the production and loved it, but it still took me the better part of a year to get re-acclimated into going to church again. This was right around the time that I started going to AA.

"There is a trait among the men in my family, and that is that we are completely honest... even to a fault. I have never known my dad, or my brother, or my son to tell a lie. And yet I was going in and out of drinking and really just being a hypocrite. I had everyone buffaloed. No one knew the extent of my problem, and some didn't even think I had one. I knew I was duplicitous, but really just didn't care.

"I stopped drinking for over a year one time. Then one night I dropped my girlfriend off, dropped my kids off, and just stopped at the liquor store and bought a pint. Two weeks later I thought, 'That was harmless. I'll do it again.' The time between each episode got shorter and shorter until I was worse off than before.

"Those are the stories you hear in AA and they are the stories you disregard because you think you're different. Don't tell a hardcore drunk that the outcome will be the same because he'll try to prove you wrong."

It was at this point in Siefken's journey that a new detour arrived. He says, "I had been shaking real badly since the late '90s. I had a titanium disc put in my C6 vertebrae because of degeneration. In 2006, I thought my tricep was extremely weak. It turns out I had degeneration of the nerves. I shook most of the time, particularly in my right hand, and I thought that was because of the nerve damage. In October of that year, my shaking became more pronounced. If I came to church, I had to sit on my hand to stop the shaking and save myself from embarrassment.

"I went to a neuro specialist, and he told me it was not Parkinson's. He gave me some meds for tremors. Shortly thereafter, I was at a conference in Tucson, walking through the airport, and I noticed that every once in a while my foot would catch on the ground. I would kind of stumble. It was then that I knew this was spreading to my leg.

"I talked to a number of people, and ended up going to Mayo Clinic. I sat there for four and a half days before they could get me in. They did a barrage of tests and said, 'We think you've got Parkinson's, but there's no way through any tests that we can definitively say you have it. What we can do is prescribe as if you had Parkinson's, and if your conditions abate or disappear, then we know you have it. If that doesn't work, then you have something else.'

"When they put me on these meds, in less than two weeks the symptoms largely went away. I did a lot of studying on Parkinson's and realized there are a lot of things associated with it. They call it a 'snowflake disease', because it manifests itself in myriad ways specific to the individual.

A very high percentage of people with Parkinson's, perhaps even 80% to 90%, become depressed. Anxiety is another very common trait.

"This gave me another excuse to resume drinking. The tough guy in me didn't allow for any pity-seeking. I really did have a lot to be upbeat about. I had quit my job as a stockbroker and was self-employed as a security fraud expert witness. I also served as an arbitrator for what then was called the NASD (National Association of Security Dealers), an independent securities regulator whose chief role is to protect investors by maintaining the fairness of the U.S. capital markets. These were two things I was really fired up about and business was good.

"Then came a confluence of things. I really loved the job, but who wants to hire an expert witness who has Parkinson's and is shaking and sometimes drinking. With Parkinson's, you'll have bad days where you'll be confused and unable to remember anything. It was at this point that I started to question whether or not I wanted to live."

On a Friday night in October of 2007, Doug Siefken hit bottom. He explains, "I thought I would go out and get myself some vodka and do a little drinking. Then I would hit the gym on Saturday so I would be nice and sober and not smell like booze when I went to church on Sunday. Well, instead that turned into what amounted to a four-day bender. During those four days, there was no eating. I don't remember large parts of the ordeal. Apparently, I called a girlfriend up and she called the church.

"She and I had discussed suicide before. When we would read about someone shooting themselves in their garage or hanging themselves in their basement, I'd tell her I wouldn't do it that way. I said I would go to a town and hour or two away and check into a motel and do it there.

"But the Lord was watching out for me. I got a phone call from a pastor at Northwoods, who had to know I was drunk. I got off the phone from him as quickly as possible, and I knew someone would probably be coming over so I got in my car and drove to Galesburg, a town 45 minutes from Peoria.

"I checked into a motel there. I had already drunk over a fifth of vodka that day. I can handle booze pretty well, but when you're not eating and you're dehydrated it doesn't dilute in your system. I also took somewhere between 40 and 60 anti-anxiety meds and mixed them with another quart of vodka.

"I knew that drinking when you're taking those anti-anxiety meds can increase the efficacy or enhance their power by three to five times. I think it's probably safe to say that it's a miracle I'm even alive today.

"Also, I didn't have anything to slit my wrists, other than a razor I had brought along. I tried to cut my wrists, but obviously didn't get the vein or I wouldn't be here today. When I woke up in the morning, and I wasn't expecting to wake up, the bed was full of blood.

"I was tremendously hung over, but I got in the car and drove to Peoria. I pulled into my garage, and some guys from my small group were right there two or three minutes later. They were shocked when they saw me. Another friend came over, and they all said, 'You're going into the hospital whether you like it or not.' I agreed.

"I was in the loony bin for six days. It's pure hell to be there. I had people come to visit, but when Cal Rychener came by, his demeanor was different than that of the others. He seemed neither shocked nor accusatory. He asked me several pointed questions and then said, 'When you get out of here, come see me and we're going to get you cleaned up. I want to know what the real Doug Siefken looks like.'

"I really appreciated that.

"When I did get out, I was just extremely embarrassed. I didn't want to go to the gym or even to church. I had a special appointment to see some trained prayer counselors at Northwoods and Cal said, 'When that's over, come and see me.' They didn't have enough Kleenex to accommodate the crowd that night. Guys from my small group were there and my daughter was there. While I was embarrassed, I still felt okay around those people.

"I was a wreck. Even though I was crying, I knew it wasn't a bad thing to cry in front of people. I'm sure the people praying for me were relieved to see my tears as it showed appreciation, vulnerability, and life. I'll never forget their outpouring of love.

"After the prayer session, I went over to Cal's office and he led me through a time of freedom ministry where we closed the door on some spiritual strongholds in my life.

"I truthfully do not know how it happened, but from that day forward I've been a different man and have pursued a life of both sexual purity and sobriety. It's a very odd thing. Every time I drive around town, I pass places... liquor stores, homes, apartments, bars... places I've sinned... and think 'What the heck were you doing!'

"It was difficult to deal with the embarrassment of failed suicide, but the Lord became my sanctuary and my refuge.

"The simple reality is that if you were in people's closets at night listening to what goes on, you would learn that everyone has problems. The fact that God brought mine into the open was His way of letting me hit bottom. He had to let me self-destruct. Sure, He could have stepped in and intervened at any time. He could have let me die.

"I know mine was a serious attempt at suicide. It wasn't just a cry for help. The booze was part of the confluence. It provided the courage. As stupid as that sounds, it gave me the courage to try and commit suicide."

As Siefken embraced sobriety, he began to see that he was part of God's plan. He says, "There were things that happened that were, to say the least, unusual. Over the years, I've been a big hunter with my brother and my dad. I loved to hunt, but I didn't really enjoy cleaning the guns. When I attempted suicide, I honestly thought my guns were over at my brother's place being cleaned. They weren't. They were a few feet away from me in my house. If I had remembered that, I would have used them.

"A couple of weeks after I got out of the loony bin, I was at church on a Saturday night with my daughter. I told her I was a little embarrassed to be seen anywhere. She laughed and said, 'Man up! You did it. Now own it.' Because of her, I forced myself to get back out in public. I figured, 'Hey, I'm still here. This has only enhanced my story!'"

Not only is Doug still here, but over the last few years he has developed an insatiable appetite for the Bible, for studying archaeology and apologetics and seeking to convince any who will listen of the reality of who God is and what He can do in your life.

The Doug Siefken you find today is still exuberant, but he's now focused on things eternal. He says, "What's important to me now in my walk with God is my kids. At this point, I am 100% convinced of Christ's existence and His authority. To walk with Christ, the first thing you do is bring yourself to a 'no doubt' place. Then you pursue the assignment Jesus gave us in the Great Commission (Matthew 28: 19-20), which is to help others come to know Him. That really needs to start at home. At this point, you need to hone your skills because you're so eager to share what you feel. The peace of God that you feel is something you want everyone to know.

"I pray every night that God will reveal Himself to my kids. I get this feeling, and I know it's from God, that my kids are going to be okay and that they will be saved. I didn't hear an audible voice, but I know the feeling came from Him.

"I am so serious about wanting my kids to know the Lord that I have written them a letter stating evidence to prove that Jesus was who He said He was. When I started the letter, I figured I could get all my thoughts in about 10 pages. Not so. I'm up over 150 pages and still writing.

"It's fascinating to me that there has never been an archaeological find that disputes even one item in the New Testament. This stuff is more than fascinating. It's compelling evidence.

"I look at it this way. If there truly is an eternity, don't you think we owe it to ourselves to invest the time and effort to find out if God and His promises are real?"

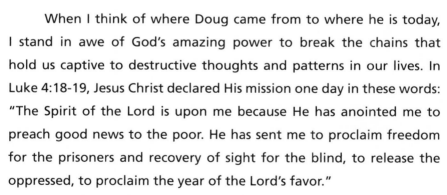

When I think of where Doug came from to where he is today, I stand in awe of God's amazing power to break the chains that hold us captive to destructive thoughts and patterns in our lives. In Luke 4:18-19, Jesus Christ declared His mission one day in these words: "The Spirit of the Lord is upon me because He has anointed me to preach good news to the poor. He has sent me to proclaim freedom for the prisoners and recovery of sight for the blind, to release the oppressed, to proclaim the year of the Lord's favor."

For years, I knew only that Jesus Christ had come to preach the good news of salvation. That essentially meant that He had come to forgive sin and offer eternal life to all who would believe. As precious as those gifts are, I now realize that it wasn't the whole story of the good news He came to offer.

Included in that good news is the powerful reality that He also frees prisoners (people who are bound by physical, mental and emotional chains and addictions) and releases the oppressed (people who are under the influence and torment of the evil one). Over the last several years, I have seen many people, like Doug, come into the glorious freedom that Jesus Christ came to bring. He can and will set you free if you'll open your life to Him and invite Him to do His work in you.

Making Music Again

Julie's Story

*"Mother had talent that was never developed, a music box
that was never allowed to play, a career that was never begun.
Mother died with the music still in her."*

SILVER BOXES BY FLORENCE LITTAUER

John Eldredge, in his book *Waking the Dead*, writes, "There is a glory to your life that your enemy fears and is hell-bent on destroying before you can act on it." He adds, *"The story of your life is the story of a long and brutal assault on your heart by the one who knows what you could be and fears it."*

Now mind you, that assault doesn't usually come in direct attacks upon our hearts; they can be very subtle attacks and they don't usually come in malicious ways. They are messages that we pick up along the way that cause us to doubt the very strengths and dreams that God has put in our hearts.

A lot of times those messages come from people who truly care about us and who simply have no idea that the unintended message they are conveying is squelching something deep within us. But once we accept those messages, they have a way of crippling us right at the very place of our greatest strengths. Consequently, we shut off those places in our hearts and then go through life feeling like the real us is locked up somewhere inside our body.

For many years, Julie Walker felt like the "real Julie" was locked up inside her — until God set her free to be who He had made her to be all along. Julie's story reminds us that God has a purpose and a plan for each of our lives and we will only feel fully alive to the extent that we pursue and embrace who He has made us to be. Her story is a reminder that God can empower you to reach the destiny He intended for you.

On any typical summer afternoon in the early 1980s, neighbors in the East Bluff neighborhood of Peoria, Illinois, might have opened their screen doors to the sight of a 7-year-old little girl asking, "Would you like to come over and hear me sing?"

Of those long-ago childhood days, Julie (Westendorf) Walker says, "I loved singing and performing. I was very confident when I was a little girl. I would plan backyard performances where I would go door-to-door through our neighborhood, personally inviting our neighbors to hear me sing. I sang at every family gathering and performed for my parents every night before I went to bed."

One might wonder where Julie got her love of music in the first place, because it's basketball, not song, that flows through her veins. Her maternal grandfather, Dick Van Scyoc, coached high school basketball for 45 years before retiring with 826 wins and a state championship under his belt. He is one of the winningest coaches in Illinois history, has been inducted into the Illinois Basketball Coaches Association Hall of Fame, and earned eight Coach of the Year awards. He was the 1991 Tri-County Sports Figure of the Year and is one of the 100 Legends of IHSA Boys Basketball.

Julie's father, Chuck Westendorf, worked for 35 years as a high school assistant coach, head coach, and athletic director. He amassed six state titles, more than any other coach in the state, and is a member of the Illinois Basketball Coaches Association Hall of Fame... although he did once lose a sectional title to Julie's grandpa!

According to Julie, "Any child who loves sports would have loved growing up as part of my family. We attended sporting events throughout the week and every weekend. My father, grandfather, and uncle were all basketball coaches, and both my sister and I were introduced to the sport at a very early age. Although I liked watching sports, I was not an athlete, and that was very apparent."

Such was not the case for Julie's sister, Joy, who was a mere 13 months older than her. Julie says, "She was an excellent basketball player. The better Joy got at basketball, the more attention she received wherever we went. I remember one time in particular when a person turned to us in church and said, 'Which one's the star?'

"Dad quickly responded, 'They're both stars,' but that comment deeply hurt me. It was as if I did not exist, and feelings of inferiority began to take root. I knew it bothered my parents when people would make such comments, and I was always grateful when they stood up for me.

"As a child, I virtually lived in a gym. Between my grandfather and my father's coaching, as well as my sister's games, it seemed like we were in a gymnasium every night. My parents tried getting me involved in different sports, but I wasn't very good and really didn't enjoy it. Looking back, I believe it was the constant comments made to my sister by other adults in front of me that left me feeling like I was not good enough. I started internalizing feelings of unworthiness because I was not good at basketball, the one sport my entire family loved and was completely consumed by.

"My dad always said that if he had a dime for every time someone would ask which one of his kids was the basketball player, he would be a rich man. I believe this was the cause of my loss of confidence."

By the time Julie reached the sixth grade and had her first chance to try out for a school music program, the once-enthusiastic little girl who had invited her neighbors to hear her sing had been replaced by a less confident, more anxious version of herself. However, she summoned the courage to audition and landed the role of the Tin Man in the school production of *The Wizard of Oz*.

In retrospect, she laughs about this role. "I walked around for three days in the most awful metal contraption of a costume. It took two people to get me in it, and I couldn't sit down once it was on. I must have really wanted the part, because no one else would have been able to endure that costume!"

The experience was worth it, though, because it helped guide her parents to The Children's Community Theater, where she auditioned and received a part in *Pirates of Penzance*. Julie says, "The directors were very encouraging and informed my parents that I was talented and should continue on this path."

In spite of their own limited exposure to theater, Julie's parents were happy to see their daughter beginning to find her own place, and they were very supportive, attending her practices and performances.

As she entered the seventh grade, a local school, Roosevelt Magnet, became a performing arts school, and Julie decided to attend. "Looking back," Julie says, "my two years at Roosevelt Magnet were the two best years of schooling in my life. The music and drama teachers encouraged my parents and me to continue pursuing the performing arts."

Even though she was surrounded by encouraging teachers and supportive parents, Julie couldn't shake the feelings of unworthiness that had already started to take root. She says, "Although I loved attending Roosevelt, I barely had any confidence to audition for musicals. When I auditioned and landed a part, it still wasn't enough to boost my poor self-image. Even with the successes I was having, I just couldn't rise above my low self-esteem."

For her ninth grade year, Julie attended Woodruff High School, where she made wonderful friends, was elected secretary of her class, and joined the show choir group. But soon, she says, "basketball won out." Her grandfather was the head basketball coach at Manual, another Peoria area high school. Her father was the assistant coach there, and after Julie's freshman year, her mother got a job at Manual as well. Her sister was excited about the possibility of playing for the girls' basketball team there, so both sisters transferred schools.

The transition was hard for Julie. She remembers, "I disliked attending Manual so much that at the end of my sophomore year, my parents began researching alternative schools for me. We were directed to check out the North Carolina School of the Arts upon the recommendation of other educators. We drove to NCSA for an audition and I was accepted. I spent the rest of the summer preparing to attend an out-of-state school. When we left for school in August, three hours into the drive, I became so anxious that I had a change of heart and said, 'I can't leave. I can't do this.'

"My mom was apprehensive too, so she turned the car around and we came home. Even today, I still wonder what might have happened if I had attended NCSA.

"I returned to Manual for my junior year and tried to survive in a less than encouraging atmosphere. I was still involved in the school plays, choirs, and musicals. I remember that the student body could pay $2 to attend the musical productions at school. Students would literally pay to get out of class and would be extremely loud and rude during our shows. For instance, I remember the students in the audience throwing Skittles® at us while we were on stage performing. It was not fun and I couldn't wait to graduate and be done with high school."

For college, Julie decided to attend Indiana University in Bloomington, Indiana. She says, "Not only did it have a prestigious music school, but also Bobby Knight was the head basketball coach, and my dad was extremely excited for me."

At the beginning of her sophomore year, Julie auditioned for The Singing Hoosiers, an elite show choir to which very few underclassmen were accepted. During her audition, the director asked her to sing *The Star Spangled Banner*. After hearing it performed at thousands of basketball games over the years, it should have been ingrained in her memory by then.

But, she says, "I started the National Anthem and partially into the song, completely forgot the words. The director was really nice and told me to stop and regain my composure before starting again. I took a deep breath, started singing, and simply could not remember the words. I was mortified and knew I had just blown the opportunity.

"I went back the next day to see who had made the group and found my name on the list. I could not believe it. Being part of The Singing Hoosiers was a great experience, but to this day I am afraid to sing the National Anthem."

———··◁∞▷··———

At the end of her sophomore year, Julie decided that Indiana University was not for her. Around the same time, she received a call from the Director of Music at Rollins College in Winter Park, Florida, which had been her second choice for college two years earlier. The director informed Julie that Rollins had a new music scholarship and asked her to fly down to audition for it. She was accepted to school, became the first recipient of the very generous scholarship, and transferred to Rollins for her junior and senior years.

At Rollins, Julie had another run-in with both basketball and *The Star-Spangled Banner*. During her senior year, she was part of a musical trio that sang at various events — one being a big televised college basketball game, which was played before a sellout crowd of 60,000 fans in the Orlando Magic arena. Finding strength in numbers, Julie thought she could overcome her nervousness as part of a trio. But at the last minute, one member of the trio was not able to make it. Both Julie and the other member said they couldn't do it without the whole group.

According to Julie, "The person in charge of the arena said, 'Someone from Rollins has got to go out there and sing.' The only person who could sing alone was the soprano and, of course, I was the soprano! I remember thinking this couldn't be happening. When the moment came to go to the center of the court, someone gave me a little push, and I nervously strolled out onto that huge arena full of people and sang the National Anthem."

Looking just at a list of Julie's musical accomplishments during high school and college, it's plain to see that she had talent. She landed choice roles in school productions and community theater.

She was chosen for elite music groups at two universities and was approached by a collegiate Director of Music himself about a generous music scholarship. She could often even sing her parts or perform without much practice, which frustrated the other vocal students. But in spite of her many accomplishments, she carried her lack of confidence into college and beyond. Simply put, Julie never thought she was good enough.

Julie says, "All through my college career, I completely lacked confidence and had to fight myself to even audition for things that I loved." Interestingly enough, in her life outside of music, Julie had plenty of friends and didn't struggle to stand up for herself. Her greatest gift had also become her greatest struggle.

Julie (Westendorf) Walker was raised in a church, but she and her parents became Christ-followers only after finding Northwoods Community Church. At the end of college, she returned to Peoria and joined her parents as regular attenders of Northwoods.

She wanted to get involved with the music ministry, but her lack of courage and confidence held her back. Even after finally working up the nerve to talk to the music director and committing to sing for a weekend service, she backed out several times because of her insecurity.

"I simply couldn't understand it," she says. "I prayed and prayed and pleaded with God to tell me why I was feeling this way. It was just horrible that I would become so exhausted about singing that I could barely function. Sometimes my mouth would become extremely dry or I would break out in hives or have horrible stomachaches. My heart would beat out of my chest. Singing was my passion and I just couldn't do it."

Finally, though, God gave Julie the strength to sing onstage at Northwoods. The worship team prayed with her before every service she sang in to help her overcome her fears. She always felt great once she was on stage singing, and she felt good afterwards too, knowing that she had overcome her fears. Slowly, the anxiety lessened with each time she was on stage, but the weekends that she was on stage were always stressful for her, and she was always exhausted from that stress when the weekends she sang were over.

Many other aspects of her life had become difficult as well. Five years into their marriage, Julie and her husband Donny received the happy news that she was pregnant with their first child. She says, "Everyone in our family was so excited because this would be the first grandchild on both sides of our family. Then, three months into the pregnancy, I miscarried. I was devastated and really questioned God."

Four months later, Julie learned that she was pregnant again. She put the tiny life inside her into God's hands. She says, "I had the prayer team at Northwoods pray over me, and I just knew I would carry this baby to full term. I cannot explain it any other way than to say I felt God speaking to me and assuring me that my prayer would be answered."

On May 6, 2004, Julie gave birth to a healthy baby boy, her son Weston. The Walkers were overjoyed by his birth.

But this joy preceded another period of grief. In quick succession, Donny Walker lost his mother and both of his grandmothers. Then Julie miscarried a second time, and then a third.

She says, "After my third miscarriage, we were referred to a specialist in Chicago because we really wanted another child and we were still suffering from all the loss we had endured. The doctors ran many tests, and the bottom line was I was unable to carry a baby to full term. They had no idea how I was ever able to have Weston. To us, Weston is a complete miracle, and we are now extremely happy and overjoyed that God blessed us with a healthy baby boy!"

Meanwhile, Julie held a few years of non-music jobs in the Peoria area. She says, "All the while, I was wondering how music could ever become part of my vocation. After three years of answering telephones and a stint in development and fundraising, I felt unfulfilled. I was searching and praying for God's direction in my life. I just believed that God had something different planned for me, something that would involve music. Every Sunday, I received so much inspiration and hope from the messages I heard. My mom and I would talk after church and she would say, 'I don't know what my gift is, but Julie, it is so apparent that God gave you a beautiful voice so you can sing.'

"Many weekends, I would hear messages at church on being strong and using the gifts God has given you. I would be motivated and try to encourage myself to be stronger and live the life God meant for me. Finally, when I was in my late 20s, I heard a particular weekend message that ended with a story about a woman who desperately wanted to sing; but like a music box, she died with the music still inside her. I remember thinking, 'That's me! I'm going to be 80 years old and never have lived my dream and used the passion and the gift God has given me.'"

———••◁∞▷••———

Then Julie's sister, who lived in Chicago, told her about a program called Music Together. It is a music and movement program for infants through five-year-olds, based on the premise that all children are musical. Julie immediately checked it out online and thought, "Wow, this is something I can do. We have nothing like this in Peoria and this is something I can do with a baby."

Before Julie's insecurities could get the best of her, God arranged every detail perfectly. Julie explains, "One problem was that the next training session was only one week away. But that was probably a blessing because I didn't have time to talk myself out of it!

"I hate driving, especially to Chicago, but my dad took away that objection by announcing he would drive me there. I then attempted to find another way out by telling myself this trip would be too expensive. However, I bargained with God and told Him if He could find me a deluxe hotel on Priceline for $45 a night, I would have no choice but to go. Priceline instantly charged my credit card and I was booked into a suite at the DoubleTree! After the training, my husband found a great spot for me to rent in downtown Peoria and my music business really came together.

"I started Music Together in the summer of 2005 with 10 paying families. All the while, I was attending Northwoods and hearing positive messages of encouragement. I was constantly praying that my new endeavor would work out.

"That summer was the first time in my life I ever tithed. I'm not proud to admit it, but it's the truth. I had no idea how I was going to cover my business expenses and rent but felt a prompting to tithe. The day that I made that decision, I got a phone call from someone with twins, asking if they could sign up even though it was past the deadline. Their tuition was the exact sum of money that I had tithed to church. God is so faithful!

"I jumped from 10 families in the summer to over 50 families and seven classes in the fall. The same thing happened again. As I wrote a check for my tithe, I got calls from people wanting to sign up late. Again, I was just overwhelmed with how God was working in my life."

Her business grew, her faith grew, her confidence grew, and her dreams grew. But even though she loved Music Together and the connections she was able to make with families through music, Julie still felt that she was missing something on a personal level.

Because Music Together is a franchise, she was only able to follow their program guidelines. However, through the program, she was singing in front of people every day and gaining more confidence.

Then Northwoods did a series entitled *The Bucket List*. The series encouraged attenders to seize their dreams. Julie felt that she had been "ejected out of her seat." For her entire life, she had dreamed of creating her own children's album. On the Monday after the service, in August of 2008, she set about making this dream a reality.

She called a local music producer, Brett James, and they began working on an album with songs she had written. She says, "As Brett and I collaborated, my music came to life, and I began to feel more confident and sure of my direction.

"Throughout this process, I prayed and asked God to direct me daily, and I found that my confidence continued to grow. While working on the album, I heard God speak to me about selling my business. My family thought I was absolutely crazy because I had a successful enterprise that seemed to really fit my gifting. It was something I couldn't really explain to anyone. I moved forward with my decision, as I felt confident God had prompted me to do this.

"My first album, *A Sunny Day*, was finally released in September 2009, while I was completing my last semester of teaching Music Together. It was an emotional time for me as my classes came to an end and I embarked on a new journey. In my heart, I felt I was doing the right thing, but the unknown can be scary."

Julie Walker's new endeavor has been greeted with success from the start. She held an album release party in November of 2009 to celebrate her new career as a musical entertainer for children and families. She says, "I was just hoping that at least 20 people would attend. I was overcome with emotion when the venue was filled to capacity! I felt so much love and support from all the families who attended. It was just another confirmation from God that He was holding my hand and leading me down this path."

Julie K Music, where Julie uses her first name and middle initial, has secured musical venues throughout the Midwest. She has done a fundraiser for a national organization as well as a televised performance. The album has even won several national awards, including a 2010 *Dr. Toy's Best Vacation Product Award*, a 2010 *Parents' Choice Award*, and a *Dove Family Approved* seal. Julie has Bible verses that correspond to every song, so she ties her performances to children's ministry.

The Westendorf family supports Julie every step of the way, and her mother serves as Julie's personal assistant and booking agent. After years of uncertainty, all the pieces have finally fallen into place. Julie says, "I still sometimes question myself, but whenever I do, God seems to make something positive happen."

One example of this came exactly a year after the debut of her *A Sunny Day* album. In September of 2010, Julie was asked to sing at a reading event hosted by Congressman Aaron Schock. Former First Lady Laura Bush was in attendance. Julie used to regret that due to her husband's job as a firefighter, she could not move outside of the Peoria city limits. Now she rejoices at how God brings the opportunities to her!

Regarding the future of Julie K Music, she says, "I don't know where all this is going to lead, but I'm trusting God to guide me each and every day. I know He wants me to rely on Him. If I can sing and glorify Him, then I believe I am fulfilling my purpose. We're booking events, I have already released my second album, and every day is an exciting adventure.

"I just feel for all these years, I've had this music locked up inside me, and now, I am finally able to share it. My prayer for a long time has been, 'Please God, give me the confidence I had when I was a little girl.'

"Through prayer and Bible study, I've come to learn and accept that God has given me this voice and He's not going to let me fail. So much of my release has come from really just giving it over to God. Giving up my desire to be in control has absolutely been huge. I may only be taking baby steps, but I know that He is progressing me at His pace, wanting to see and know that I will be faithful.

"Everyone who had anything to do with my album project was from Northwoods Community Church, including the design of my logo and website. Sometimes I have to wonder: if my parents had never attended Northwoods, would I have ever found my way here? Would my music still be locked somewhere inside me? All I know is that I did something I thought was impossible. I now know Matthew 19:26 to be true. As Jesus said, 'With man this is impossible, but with God, all things are possible!'"

The story that so inspired Julie was told by author Florence Littauer about her mother-in-law, Marita Littauer. After knowing her for many years and being a little intimidated by her, Florence one day asked the aging woman what she would have been if she could have been anything she wanted. Marita answered without hesitation, "An opera singer! I wanted to study music, but my parents felt that was a waste of time, that I'd make more money in the millinery business. But I was in one show in college, and I had the lead."

Florence writes, "The memory of that dream never left Marita Littauer, even though her mother had shot it down. In her last days, her mind faded and she could no longer speak. But some evenings she would stand proudly by her chair and sing opera to her nurse. Even in the twilight of her years, that deep desire never left her."

Then Florence concludes with these haunting words: "Mother had talent that was never developed, a music box that was never allowed to play, a career that was never begun. Mother died with the music still in her."

"Mother died with the music still in her." Something about that line and the imagery of this aged woman standing by her chair singing opera in the twilight of her life, nearly brings me to tears every time I read it. How many people reach the end of their lives only to realize that they never really released what was inside them all along?

Friend, don't let that happen to you! God can and will do amazing things through you if you'll release your fears to Him and by faith, step out to seize the plan and purposes He has for you.

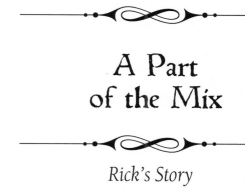

A Part of the Mix

Rick's Story

"In the beginning, there was darkness. No church, no spiritual guidance, no God. I had distrust and distaste for religion. My life was out of control."

RICK JEREMIAH

A few weeks ago at a leader's gathering in Chicago, I had the chance to catch up with a fellow pastor whom I've known for nearly 20 years but whom I rarely see except for the few times over the intervening years that I've run into him at events such as these.

He asked me if I would drive him to his hotel after the event, and I gladly obliged. During our brief time together, I remarked that I barely recognize him today compared to what he looked like when I first met him years ago. Then, he was overweight and out of shape. Today, he's the picture of health and fitness.

I would guess that he carries at least 80 pounds less on his 5'9" frame than he did 20 years ago. The wire-rim glasses he used to wear have been replaced by contact lenses. His hair, his face, his over-all appearance have changed so dramatically that I would not have recognized him had I not known his name. It would be accurate to say that this pastor has undergone an amazing physical transformation.

But even more amazing to me is when someone undergoes a radical spiritual transformation. While they may still look the same on the outside, they are so different on the inside that everything about their attitude, demeanor, speech, and behavior render them almost unrecognizable when compared to their former condition.

Rick Jeremiah is one such person. When I see him walking with the Lord and serving Him today, I just shake my head in wonderment at the amazing transformation that has taken place in his life. Rick's story is a reminder that God can radically change the life of anyone who puts his faith fully in Jesus Christ.

"My story might best begin in a hospital room. It was there that I developed a real distaste for religion while watching a nun pray over a man in a hospital bed next to my father. It was late at night and my father was dying. I was sitting in the corner of a darkened two-bed ward, and as I watched this, I remember thinking, 'Why did she pray over him?'

"She entered the room in the dark of night with her flashlight and checked wristbands. Then she prayed over the one guy, but she didn't pray for my father.

"Later during that night I asked the nurse, 'What's the deal with the nun and the flashlight and the praying over one of these men but not the other?' She kind of shrugged her shoulders and explained that the nun had been looking to see if there was a 'C' or a 'P' on the wristband. If the wristband had a 'C', she would pray for the Catholic patient.

"The thought I was left with at this difficult time was 'God must be pretty darned selective.'"

That story took place in 1975, when Rick Jeremiah was 23 years old. His father's wristband was labeled with a "P" for Protestant, although Rick describes his actual background as "non-religious." He says, "God wasn't part of our daily lives. As children, we never had Sunday school or church in our lives. You would think with no religious background that I would have been more calloused to the kind of scene that night in the hospital, but obviously I wasn't because it made a long and lasting impression."

By the time that Rick sat by his father's hospital bed, he knew "the reality was that my life was already spinning out of control." He had married shortly after graduating from high school, and the young couple faced challenges from the beginning. At the age of 18, Rick Jeremiah began to work on a crew for the railroad, which meant that he spent most of his time away from his young wife.

He says, "I was the youngest crew member and was surrounded by 40- and 50-year-old guys. It is an understatement to say there were absolutely no moral values in that group. There were certainly no role models on a daily basis to keep me centered."

In spite of the challenges, Rick did try his hardest in the beginning. His first son was born in 1976, when Rick was 25 years old. His second son followed a year later, in 1977. Rick labored hard to support his growing family. And on the railroad, working hard meant long hours.

He says, "At that time, we would work 12 hours straight and end up in Logansport, Indiana, where we would spend the night, and then come back to East Peoria the next day. Most of our 8 or 10 hours off were spent hanging out at a bar. This, of course, led to issues with drinking.

"You pretty much had to drink if you were a railroader. Alcohol was your survival mechanism. You would work 12 hours, get drunk, and try to forget that you were spending your life on the road. Being in bars that much connects you to other lonely people and leads to lots of one-night stands."

For Rick, these one-night stands started in 1979, when he had been married eight years.

He says, "I knew I wasn't doing the right thing, but I didn't care. I had nothing to center me and drag me away. That lifestyle and that behavior spun on and on for the 19 years I worked for the railroad."

During those days, alcohol and daily life went hand-in-hand. Rick remembers, "I would drive to Logansport every Sunday afternoon with another guy. I would pick him up in Washington, Illinois, and we would grab a case of beer. The two of us would consume the entire case driving from Washington to Watseka. That's 80 miles. Then we would buy a 12 pack to make it the last 60 miles to Logansport. In our minds, we were never drunk."

Another time, Rick remembers driving back from Indiana late on a Saturday night after working a 12-hour shift. He remembers stopping at the westbound stop sign in El Paso, then proceeding west. After that, he doesn't remember anything until coming up out of the valley at Panther Creek, two miles later on curving roads.

He says, "I shudder now to think of those days. We were so crazy, so stupid, and so immature. God had to be looking out for me, because surely nobody else was. He was also protecting everybody else on the road from my stupidity."

Then, in 1989, life as Rick knew it underwent some changes — though not necessarily for the better.

He says, "When I was 37 years old, they closed our branch of the railroad, and I was laid off. Then I was forced to spend all my time with my wife, a woman I didn't even know. It was an interesting time, but ultimately it led to divorce. We grew up not really knowing each other, and then we were forced together. I had been an absentee husband with a whole life outside of the family.

"I didn't know how to cope. We survived for awhile and eventually I got another job, but then the cycle repeated itself. I would go to work and stop for a few beers on the way home. I went right back to having one-night stands. When my wife found out about one of them, that was it.

"Between me never being home and the alcohol and the affairs, it was finally just over. No one could ever blame her for having had enough of my behavior. One of the things I struggle with, now that I have my life centered and know right from wrong, is what I did to that woman and the pain I put her through.

"Fortunately she moved on and found another man, remarried, and appears to be happy. We still have contact because of our involvement with our sons and grandchildren, and we don't beat each other up about the sins of our past lives, although I should probably be beaten on a regular basis for putting her through so much pain."

Rick and his wife divorced in 1990, after 22 years of marriage. Shortly thereafter, he began to date a woman who worked in the same office as him, and they were married in 1991, six months after his divorce. Soon, though, Rick began to fall back into his old patterns. He says, "I tried to stray and she could sense it. She knew my background and really unloaded on me."

Rick remembers that in those early days of his second marriage, he could be "rather irritating," so he and his new wife had some big fights. He says, "I would wait for the alarm clock to finally go off so I could take a shower, go to work, and get away from it. Then we would start right back up at 5:30 when I got home. We had running battles, sometimes two days long.

"But despite all that, we loved each other and didn't want to repeat the errors we had made in our first marriages. We had each grown in different directions than our spouses and knew how that played out. In the back of our minds was always the thought that we didn't want to be labeled a 'rebound couple.'"

It didn't take long for the new Mrs. Jeremiah to realize that something needed to change. She had attended Sunday School and Vacation Bible School as a child, but had moved away from church as she had gotten older. When a girlfriend invited her to visit Northwoods Community Church, she accepted, and as Rick says, "It wasn't long after going to church that she reconnected with Jesus Christ. She simply realized pretty quickly that something significant was missing from her life."

Rick, however, was extremely cynical about church in general, and Northwoods Community Church in particular. He says, "I would make fun of her for going to church. I'd tell her that I heard they pumped gas into Northwoods. Otherwise, how else could they make people that happy? I constantly told her something funny had to be going on out there."

But Rick's wife remained undeterred. She continued attending Northwoods and praying for her husband.

Rick says, "When the atrium and expanded children's facilities were being built, they had a ceremony after a mid-week service where they wrote people's names on construction stakes and drove those stakes in the ground in the outline of the building. This was basically a prayer to get the people who were named on the stakes to come to know Christ. I didn't know until later that she had written my name on a stake.

"Shortly after that, she finally talked me into at least driving her to the building and then picking her up after services. I would begrudgingly get up on Sunday morning, drive her to church, and then go have coffee somewhere. She would call me when the service was letting out, and I would come back to the front door and slow down long enough for her to hop in.

"After a while, my wife said in a rather subtle way, 'You know, they've got a coffee bar in the lobby. Nobody is going to accost you or thrust a Bible at you.'

"So she finally talked me into doing my waiting in the lobby at the coffee bar. I had to wait for the doors to open for the coffee bar to open. I would watch the doors and noticed that when they opened, the people poured out. They were all smiling and happy. Evidently I couldn't smell the mind-control gas from the lobby.

"The next thing she did was say, 'You know, there's a Wednesday night service, and it's a little more laidback. Won't you at least come and just give it a try?'

"Frankly, she just plain wore me out. Since I was bringing her to church anyway, I decided to give in and appease her. I was the stereotypical husband who didn't want to be in church. I planted myself in the seat, crossed my arms, and tried to tune everything out. I'm sure my body language said it all.

"It didn't happen all at once, but I got to the point where I liked Wednesday nights. To this day, I don't know if it was the music or the message or just the buzz in the room. But whatever it was had won me over.

"Pretty soon, I asked my wife, 'What's Sunday like?'

"'Not that different,' she said. 'It's got similar music and a longer message.'

"I told her maybe I would give Sundays a try. I started coming on Sundays and found myself softening. I don't know exactly when, but my arms uncrossed and I started paying attention to the message. I had loved the music from the very beginning, but then I noticed myself really leaning in to the message.

"I can't remember the exact weekend series, but I do know it was one of the times when Cal issued an altar call at the close of his message. He led the congregation in prayer and said, 'If you're ready to accept Christ as your Savior and welcome Jesus into your life, please stand up.'

"I stood up. I almost surprised myself. But my surprise was nothing compared to my wife and her girlfriend who was sitting next to her. They both started sobbing because they knew the prayers they had prayed and about the stake they had planted outside the church.

"It was pretty much an instantaneous decision. I like to read and had done some studying. I knew Jesus' story and that He had died on a cross. Before Northwoods, I'm not certain that I knew *why* He had died on a cross… and the *'why'* is what's ever so important to His story.

"Interestingly, even though I liked to read and had studied the beginning and the end of the Bible, I never spent much time with the New Testament. I had previously been fascinated by Revelation, and for a non-believer, that's definitely a freaky book!

"Between my days of leaving the coffee bar to enter the auditorium and actually making a statement for Christ, I had pored through the New Testament. Reading it touched my heart as I learned of the betrayal, the denial, and the crucifixion. It made me both mad and sad.

"I have always been the type of person who can weigh the evidence and make a decision and a firm commitment. My decision that day was simply, 'I need this. God knows my flaws. God knows the sin in my life. He watched me through all the years of my imperfection. He allowed His Son to die on a cross for me and for the sin I've borne over the last 20+ years. It's time to make amends.'

"I can say I have never looked back. I've never had a regret. He reminds me on a daily basis of His love, His grace, and His forgiveness.

"Because of my being stubborn, this process took some time. My wife probably attended Northwoods for a year before I even entered the building. Then once I started attending services, it took another six months before I stood up and made my commitment to Christ."

————··◁∞▷··————

"Immediately there was a little period of testing for me. I so enjoyed being at Northwoods that I wanted to be a part of it. Not long after my commitment, there was a Volunteer Expo, where the church tried to match up the various ministries with volunteers in their areas of giftedness.

"I loved what was going on in the auditorium and very much wanted to be a part of it. I had a background in sound from one of my jobs after the railroad. I signed up to be part of the technical production team and was really excited. But then I went six weeks without hearing from anyone.

"After a few weeks of not hearing anything, I heard the whispers of Satan. 'They know who you are. They don't want you.' I would hear that on a regular basis, and my only response was prayer, saying, 'Please, Lord, don't let this be the truth. I've asked You for forgiveness, and now I'm asking You to help others accept me too. Please let others see beyond my warts and flaws, just as You have done.'

"I think now that this was a test to see if I was serious about the decision I had made. God needed to know that I was really onboard with His program. I stayed true in my new faith and simply figured maybe the Northwoods' team didn't need any help. Whatever the reason, I wasn't going to stop going to church and expanding myself.

"One day, Kirk Moser, then the Technical Director, ran into me out in the Northwoods' lobby. He asked if I was Rick Jeremiah and then said, 'I owe you a huge apology. I've wanted to get with you for several weeks, but it's just been crazy around here. Can we find a time to get together and talk?'

"That conversation boosted me up to a new level of belief. I had never been a person with much self-doubt, but this was a whole new arena. It was nice to be included as a part of something so vital and energized.

"When you serve in the Creative Arts ministry at Northwoods, you hit the ground running and they build a fire in you. I took every opportunity I could to fill in whenever possible. I wasn't satisfied with just volunteering one weekend a month. I wanted it all, and I wanted it right away! I would tell people I was the luckiest guy in the world because I got to hear the message three times!"

Wanting to hear the message three times in a weekend is certainly a drastic change from Rick's old sarcastic comments about the supposed use of mind-control gas on church attenders. No longer just an observer from the coffee bar, Rick Jeremiah has come to love the Northwoods' auditorium and all that it represents.

He says, "It's where I found a safe place and finally 'got it.' That room is so special to me now, and I will protect it with my life so that other people can experience what I have experienced.

"That room is not just there for people who know God. It's also for people who don't know God and people who are sincerely searching for God. It's a safe harbor and a refuge for them to be comfortable and perhaps experience Him.

"Many of those people who are searching for God don't even know what they're looking for. I didn't know that God was missing in my life because I was running my own life. I didn't think I needed a higher power telling me what to do."

So what caused Rick to make the change from calling his own shots to giving it all over to God? He likens this change in his attitude to the flipping of a switch.

He says, "I don't really know how to describe why I knew that I was ready to accept Christ. It's as if a switch in me was turned on.

"I had been standing for the worship music since I first started attending Northwoods. In my early days, I would see people lifting their open hands during worship. I was far from ready for that, but I would notice that my hands were open down at my sides where nobody could see them. Once that switch was turned on, my hands started coming up on a regular basis.

"My new faith was so strong that on weekends when Cal would ask new believers to stand, I found myself wanting to stand all over again. My wife had to hold my hand and drag me back down. She would say, 'You've already done that! One time is all that's required.'

"Philosophically, I knew that, but I felt like I had wasted so much of my life that I needed to catch up!"

Since becoming a Christian, Rick Jeremiah has indeed worked to "catch up." He and his wife were part of Northwoods' very first lake baptism. And, he says, "We also took every class the church offered. We just couldn't get enough. Whatever they were offering, we wanted it

"I've never run a marathon, but I almost feel like I'm in one now, and I don't want to stop running. I don't want to slow down. I feel like I've missed out on so much that I want to drink it all in.

"I tell people who've known Jesus all their lives just how lucky they are. I'm not saying that I'm jealous of them because they've had more time with the Lord than I have, but I do find myself regretting the years that I missed being with Him."

———··◁∞▷··———

It is this passion for the Lord that has led Rick into full-time ministry at Northwoods. He volunteered with the sound team from the time that he accepted Christ in 2007 up until the Christmas season of 2009. He spent most of that time working professionally for the City of East Peoria as its Public Works Director, until he retired from there in 2007. His retirement only lasted for a week before he went to work for Cullinan Properties as a construction department manager. But God had other plans for him.

Rick remembers, "Just before we started into the Christmas production of 2009, the technical director had given his notice. I knew that he was leaving and that the job had been posted, but I really hadn't done anything about it or even given it much thought.

"One night during rehearsal, just before we launched the Christmas production, Dawn Henderson, the Creative Arts Director, turned to me and said, 'Rick Jeremiah, are you going to apply for that job or what?'

"I think Dawn sensed that I was interested. I looked at her and said, 'I've thought about it, but I didn't know if it would be right for me or not.'

"She said, 'Rick, you have this ministry in your heart. We can see it by the way you're always at this church and how you are the first to volunteer. I think you should try it.'

"I had no expectations of getting the job. I was one of four people who made the cut and got an interview. It just happened that I was the one who got the position.

"I told the church that I would take the job, but I had this freaky notion in my head that I owed Cullinan four to six months to finish a few things. I told Northwoods that I would gladly take the job if they would let me work it part-time while I wrapped up things with Cullinan.

"They agreed to it. That lasted two weeks. I kept hearing what I thought was my head, but was actually my heart, asking me the repeated question: 'Why are you waiting?'

"So I went home and wrote a letter to the people at Cullinan, giving them my two weeks' notice. I was certain they might ask me to leave immediately, so I had my personal belongings packed up when I gave them my letter.

"I guess God wasn't wild about me leaving so abruptly, because that afternoon, they offered me a part-time consultant's position until the end of 2010. It was all really good. I was working full-time at a place I loved and still got to have my hand in a few phases of the East Peoria re-development that I was interested in. I was putting in a lot of hours, but it was doing two things I thoroughly enjoyed."

Today, the Rick Jeremiah who works 50+ hours a week in full-time ministry is a far cry from the young railroader who used to drive those two-lane roads from Illinois to Indiana while drinking with his buddies. He is living proof that "Therefore if anyone is in Christ, he is a new creation; the old things passed away; behold, new things have come." 2 Corinthians 5:17

Rick knows that the changes in his life would never have been possible without God, as well as the specific blessings that the Lord has given him in the form of a church home and a church family.

He says, "I remember a time before I started attending church with my wife when she and I were invited out with a group of Northwoods attenders. They were all Christ-followers, and they didn't treat me any differently than anyone else. They knew my story, but it didn't matter to them. They knew I didn't go to church at Northwoods and that I struggled with my wife attending a church, but that didn't stop them from befriending me. When none of them lectured me or accosted me, it made an impression.

"Looking back, I'm so grateful that there was a place like Northwoods. I'm fairly certain that I wouldn't have survived, let alone thrived, in a traditional church setting.

"I absolutely love Northwoods. I now love my life! I love my job and the people the Lord has put into my life through this church. Being in this building is an immersion process for me. I get to witness people on staff who are role models of what Christ-followers should be. I get to see love and compassion every single day as my journey continues!"

The Bible says in 2 Corinthians 5:17, "Therefore if anyone is in Christ, he is a new creation. The old has gone, the new has come." And my friend, I want you to know that what Jesus Christ has done for Rick, He can do for you if you will invite Him to have full control of your life. I have seen him change the hardest heart.

I have seen Him break the strongest addiction. I have seen Him penetrate the darkest recesses of a person's life and bring new life. If you're wondering whether anything or anyone can change your life, I assure you God Can!

Living Through Loss

Alan & Lisa's Story

"Faith is saying I choose to believe in you, God,
more than this or that tragedy. I throw myself in utter dependence
on you – you alone, a God who specializes in resurrections,
a God who was willing to send your Son to a cross to prove
that you are more powerful than the worst thing evil could do."

PLAN B BY PETE WILSON

Okay, by this point in the book you might be thinking, "Come on, Cal. Let's get real. You can't tell me that at your church every story has a rosy ending." So let me be honest and tell you that at Northwoods, we have had our share of tragic and painful stories as well. Some difficult marriages have crashed and burned. Some prayers for healing have ended in death. Some accidents, lay-offs and painful circumstances have left people wondering why the God who can prevent such things... didn't. Some people have endured excruciating trials and wondered where God was in the midst of it all.

The truth is that none of us is exempt from real life. We live in a fallen and broken world where bad things happen to all of us. If we think that following Christ gives us an exemption clause from life's set-backs and disappointments, we're going to be sorely disappointed and awfully disillusioned when fiery trials come our way, as they will. However, every Christ-follower can live with the absolute assurance that God's promise in Romans 8:28 is true: "And we know that in all things God works for the good of those who love Him, who have been called according to His purpose."

It'd be easy to follow Christ if in doing so one was guaranteed complete protection from any and all pain in this life and nothing but success, prosperity and blessing. If that were the case, one would be crazy not to follow Him. But such is not the case in this life; that's reserved for heaven! Jesus said in John 16:33: "In this world you will have trouble. But take heart! I have overcome the world." In Psalm 91:15, God says, "I will be with you in trouble." Notice, He doesn't promise us a trouble-free existence.

That's why I believe that one of the greatest testimonies to God's love and power in the lives of His children is often seen in the midst of pain, loss, heartbreak and sorrow. When a child of God, in the midst of his tears, can yet testify to the nearness and goodness of God, the world has no explanation for it. That's why I love Alan and Lisa Heth's story. Having walked through a devastating loss too painful for words, their lives are today a powerful reminder that our God can enable you to stand when the world around you has crumbled.

--------••◦◦◦••--------

Looking back on the past decade, Alan Heth can clearly see God's hand in the events that have shaped his family's lives. He has learned to marvel at God's timing, strength, comfort, and ultimate design. And when he someday enters the gates of Heaven, he knows whose bright smile will be the first to greet him.

Alan's journey of faith began in 1999, when his family's old neighbors, Francis and Terry Cheung, returned to Dunlap, Illinois, for a weekend visit. At that time, Alan was in the car business, which he says "meant working six days a week. Sunday was my only day off, so for me that meant getting things done. That was my day for mowing the grass or golfing or any number of things I didn't have time for during the week."

The Cheungs, however, wanted to visit their old church home, Northwoods Community Church. Alan's wife Lisa and three daughters, Casey, Angela, and Alison (Ali), decided to go along. Alan remembers initially responding to their plans by saying something like, "Good for you. More power to you. I'm not going."

Shortly afterward, though, he changed his mind and got in the shower. When Lisa questioned him about it, he just said, "What the heck, everybody else is going and it won't kill me."

Alan claims that he can't remember what the message was about that day, but Lisa laughingly recounts, "That day they had a skit. It was about lying and car dealers."

In any case, Alan decided that the service was "okay." He concluded that "while the kids and Lisa were definitely more interested than me... it might even be a good thing for the family to do once in a while."

He says, "We went a couple more times in the next few months and kind of worked our way up to going semi-regularly, probably about half the time. I could see it was having a positive impact on the kids.

I remember thinking, 'This isn't all bad. It's helping them become better kids.'"

In the meantime, the car dealership that Alan had been managing was sold. After 20 years in the car business, he decided it was time for a change and he became the manager of a medical equipment distributorship. He recalls, "As time progressed, I realized that maybe I wasn't in the best situation, but I was making some money and learning a new business. I saw tons of opportunity. Then, a little over a year after I'd been with the company, I was let go.

"It came completely out of the blue. I was caught totally off-guard. I was really upset about it. I kept thinking, 'What the heck! I'm a good guy! I don't drink. I don't smoke. I don't do drugs. I don't cheat on my wife. I'm livin' a pretty good life, and here I am getting dumped on.' It really bothered me."

———— ••◄∞►•• ————

The next morning was November 6, 2001. As Alan prepared to set out on some errands, Lisa made a suggestion. She said, "If you're upset, why don't you stop at Northwoods and talk to Pastor Cal?"

The Heths' middle daughter, Angela, was the same age as Cal's oldest daughter, Kathryn, and the two girls played together on a summer league basketball team that Alan coached. Nevertheless, the two men were still largely strangers. Alan asked, "Lisa, why would I talk to Cal? I barely know the man. I've met him at basketball games and know him well enough to say 'hi.' I ask him how the church business is and he asks me how basketball is going. I have no reason to talk to that guy. I don't really even know him."

But in spite of Alan's objections, he now says that "the Holy Spirit must have hit me on the head" during his drive home from the airport.

He remembers, "I was getting this nudge of 'Go talk to him.' I was responding, 'Huh? I don't even know how to do that. Do I go to the church? Is he there? What would I say?'"

Again, the Spirit's prompting overrode Alan's objections, and he drove to the church parking lot. He continues, "As I pulled up in front of the church, Cal was out in front. So I walked up to him and said, 'Hey, can I talk to you for a few minutes?' He could probably tell in one glance that somebody needed to talk to me!

"We went into Cal's office and talked about all my feelings and how everything in my life was going great, except I had no job. I had been in the car business for 20+ years, so I had lost a lot of jobs, but this one somehow felt different.

"I gave him the same spiel I had been repeating to myself: 'I'm a good guy. I don't drink, smoke, or cheat on my wife. I love my kids. I spend time with my family. I even coach youth basketball, for Pete's sake! I've given my time!'

"Then Cal asked me a question that I'll never forget. He asked, 'How's your personal relationship with Jesus Christ?'

"I was like, 'My what? I'm supposed to have a what?' His question didn't even make sense to me. That's how foreign the concept was.

"The only thing I could say was, 'Well, I guess I don't have one.'

"Then Cal started to explain that you have to be a perfect 10 to get to God, and since none of us are, we need Jesus, because He is perfect in God's sight. Cal was talking to me about the forgiveness of sin and redemption, and I was just eating it all up.

"Suddenly, it was like the light went on and I realized, 'This makes sense!' Then I started to wonder why nobody had ever told me all of that before. After listening to Cal's explanation, I threw out the question, 'What do I have to do to get all that?'

"He said, 'Well, if you're ready, let's kneel right here and ask Jesus to become the Lord and Savior of your life.'

"I said, 'I'm all in! Let's go!' So we knelt on the floor of Cal's office, and I prayed for the forgiveness of my sins and accepted Jesus Christ as my Savior. After my prayer, we were both crying and hugging, and I was feeling great. Then Cal gave me a couple books to read and told me we would go to breakfast once a week so that he could mentor me and make sure that I got started on the right track.

"I felt like a million bucks. I was on top of the world. I had accepted Jesus and I somehow knew that everything was going to be okay.

"Then, while I was driving home, I said to myself, 'Wait, how am I going to tell Lisa? I'm going to walk through the door and she's going to say, "You did what?!"' I had to convince myself to just come out and tell her.

"So I walked in the door, and Lisa asked if I talked to Cal. I told her that I not only talked to Cal, but I also accepted Jesus Christ as my Lord and Savior. Then she started crying and I started crying. She hugged me and told me she thought that was great.

"Coming to Christ happens differently for everyone, but for me it was just like a lightning bolt out of the blue. When I got out of bed that morning, I didn't know that was what I needed, but a few hours later, I realized it all made sense and I just ran with it."

As for Lisa, she says that her own salvation story "doesn't have any bells and whistles, but I know when it happened. I always 'thought' I was a Christian. I went to church, had a Christmas tree, and believed in Jesus. Then, a few months after Alan was saved, we were at church and Cal was preaching. He was talking about crossing the line of faith and what it meant to have a relationship with Jesus. He said that simply believing in the existence of Jesus wasn't enough. He said, 'Even Satan believes in Jesus.'

"That thought struck me, and that was the day I realized that I needed a relationship with Him. And praise the Lord, I gave my life to Him, because I had no idea what I was going to come up against in the coming years."

·◦·⟨∞⟩·◦·

With both Alan and Lisa established as believers, the family became more involved in church and Bible study. Alan remembers, "At that time, the whole family started moving in the same direction. We started going to Northwoods every week and it all began making sense to me. I'd listen to messages and understand them. I'd study my Bible, and Cal mentored me at breakfast once a week. My grasp was getting stronger and my perspective was getting clearer and clearer."

At that time, the Heths' oldest daughter, Casey, was a senior at Dunlap High School. Angela was a sophomore, and Ali was in seventh grade. The girls became regular Northwoods' attenders as well.

On the professional front, Alan connected with a friend he had made in the medical equipment sales field. The man was a Christ-follower who encouraged him to get into the sales side of the business and start selling for himself. That led him into the used medical equipment business.

After graduating high school, Casey moved to Tallahassee to attend Florida State University. Both Angela and Ali continued to be involved with youth activities at Northwoods, and as Ali entered high school, she also got involved in a non-denominational Christian outreach group called Young Life. Through Young Life, she joined a small group called Campaigners for Christ. Then, when Angela was a senior and Ali was a freshman at Dunlap High School, a new opportunity arose for Alan.

He says, "I continued to work with and have contact with my friend who had encouraged me to go in the direction of used medical equipment sales. One day in 2003, he called and told me that his company had offered him a distributorship and asked if I wanted to come work for him.

"I asked if he was going north or south geographically. He kind of 'hmmmed' for a minute and then said, 'Almost straight sideways.' I said I wasn't really interested. He told me it was basically Virginia, some of Maryland, and Washington, D.C.

"Again, I said I didn't think that interested me. We had always said that if we ever left Peoria, it would be to move south. He said, 'What about Virginia Beach?' I said, 'The second word caught my attention. I think you got me interested when you said "beach."'

"I talked to Lisa and she said, 'Life's meant to be an adventure. Let's go for it!' So I actually moved out there a year before Lisa and the girls. We thought it best that Lisa stay in Dunlap and let Angela finish her senior year of high school.

"When Angela's graduation was over, we sold our house in Dunlap, packed up our belongings, and moved the family out to Virginia Beach."

Angela had decided to attend James Madison University in Harrisonburg, Virginia, approximately four hours away from her parents' new home. Ali enrolled at Kellam High School in Virginia Beach.

Lisa remembers, "When Ali and I moved to Virginia Beach, she went from Dunlap High School (which had approximately 700 students) to a school of 3,500. She had always loved basketball more than anything. But on the second day of school, she decided to give up basketball and instead signed up for Drama Club."

Alan adds, "So the kid I had toted all around the state of Illinois for six years playing youth basketball was all of a sudden in the Drama Club. I'm thinking, 'This is the coolest thing I've ever seen!' I was thrilled that she was involved in something and meeting new people."

After a while, though, it became clear to both Alan and Lisa that Ali was not happy in Virginia Beach. Alan remembers, "I don't think Ali was there very long before I realized that she needed to go back to Dunlap. That's where she was very Christ-centered. I loved her Campaigner group and the fact that she was involved and had great friends. In Virginia Beach, she was clearly pining for her Dunlap friends.

"I felt badly about taking Ali away from the life she loved. I finally talked to Lisa about it, and she was very torn. She knew she would miss her baby, but she also knew that Ali would likely be most happy back in Dunlap. Then it was a matter of figuring out the logistics. It was our plan to have Ali move back to Dunlap for second semester of her sophomore year and live with friends. Then Lisa would go back for the summer.

"We hadn't really figured out all the details for the future. We were pretty much just walking by faith. God had been good to us and had led us that far, and the details were coming together for us. He had taken me to a place with a great opportunity. Financially, we were headed in the right direction. Things were good and God was providing."

When tackling the question of where Ali would stay for the semester in Dunlap, Lisa decided to contact the parents of one of Ali's friends, Ellie Salrin, another sophomore at DHS. Lisa says, "I knew Ellie's dad was retired and Ellie was an only child, so I thought they might have extra room in their home. I knew Sue Salrin, but at the time, we were not close friends. When I look back now, I think, 'I sent my daughter back to Dunlap to live with somebody I really didn't know very well.' God had to have directed us to Sue. There was nobody better to have our daughter live with. To this day, she continues to serve me in every way."

Alan agrees, saying, "Sue went so far above and beyond what anyone could ever have asked. The first thing she did was open up her home to our daughter. She took excellent care of Ali while she was living with them and treated her like her own child. Sue just has an amazing heart. She has taken care of our family in so many ways that we could never, ever repay our debt to her. No doubt about it, she was sent to us by God."

The Heth family went back to Dunlap for a visit at Christmas time, and Alan says that they could "see in Ali's eyes that was where she was supposed to be. She was with her old friends in a place she loved. It was apparent that we were making the right choice in sending her back to Dunlap."

The family returned to Virginia Beach briefly for Ali to finish the remaining weeks of first semester. As soon as Ali's semester in Virginia Beach ended, she and her parents drove back to Dunlap and moved all of her things into the Salrins' home.

Alan remembers, "She had her own room and everything was good. She and Ellie were jumping around, hugging and chanting, 'I've got a sister! I've got a sister!'

"She had come back a couple weeks after Dunlap's semester actually began, but she quickly caught up on schoolwork. She was back in the flow with her friends and her activities. Most importantly, she was happy.

"Most parents would agree that if their children are happy, then they are happy. My saying was always, 'She only goes to high school once, but I've got her for the rest of her life.' We just didn't know how short that time would be.

"Lisa and I got in the car and drove back to Virginia Beach. I didn't have a doubt in my mind that we had done the right thing and that we had put Ali in the place she was supposed to be. It was all good!

"Three weeks later, on February 19, she was killed in a single-vehicle accident."

----•◦⟨∞⟩◦•----

"It's funny the things you remember," Alan muses. "The night the accident happened, Lisa and I were in Tallahassee, visiting Casey at Florida State University. Angela was at school at James Madison University in Virginia. Ali was with her friends and doing what she loved."

Sixteen-year-old Ali had spent the day on a Young Life sledding trip in the Quad Cities with several of her friends, including her best friend, another 16-year-old named Mary Clark.

That night, Alan says, "Lisa got a call from Sue Salrin, the mother of the friend who Ali was living with back in Dunlap. Sue told Lisa there had been a car accident (on the way home from the sledding trip) and that they didn't really know any of the details. Lisa was immediately worried, but I told her everything was going to be okay. I reasoned that if anything serious had happened, they would have Life Flighted the girls to the hospital and we'd be getting lots of details."

To all of the Heths, the situation seemed surreal. After all, they had just talked to Ali. She had called Casey only 20 minutes before the accident had happened. She had reported that they had finished their dinner break at McDonald's and were on their way back home.

Hoping to soothe everyone's nerves, Alan volunteered to call the hospital, certain that he would receive reassuring news. He remembers, "I tried to call the Emergency Room and couldn't get anyone to answer the phone, or I would get put on hold and nobody would come back to talk to me. I started to get a feeling that something a little weird was going on.

"Eventually a nurse got on the phone and said she was going to let me talk to a state trooper. That heightened my sense that something wasn't right, especially when he never got on the line.

"After what seemed like forever, we got a phone call from Chuck Weaver, whose daughter was in the van with Alison. I think I had talked to Chuck once or twice in my life. He is the one who told us that Ali and Mary had been killed in the accident.

"My immediate response was 'You've got to be kidding!' I don't know if that's how most people would respond when they learn that their child had been killed, but to me it was just so impossible that it had to be a mistake or a bad joke.

"To this day, I can't thank Chuck enough. How do you make a phone call like that? I'm sure it was painful for him to do, but he did it. This was at a time when I couldn't get anybody else to talk to me. He'll probably never know how much I appreciate him doing something that I know was really, really hard for him."

Alan learned that Ali and her friend, Mary Clark, had been killed in a single-vehicle accident on the way home from their Young Life sledding outing. The driver of their 12-passenger van lost control on eastbound Interstate 74 in Knox County with snowy roads. The van slid off the road and rolled, ending up on the westbound lane of I-74 on its driver side. Mary and Ali were found partially outside the van. Although Mary and Ali were wearing seatbelts, they both died of head injuries at the scene. The five other occupants of the vehicle, some seatbelted and some not, received minor injuries, at best.

It was up to Alan to share this information with his wife and two remaining daughters. He remembers, "When I got off the phone with Chuck, Lisa and Casey were both staring at me and dreading what I would say. They could tell from my expression that it wasn't good. As soon as I said, 'Ali and Mary have been killed in a car accident,' they let loose with screams and great crying.

"My first reaction was 'We've got to pray.' So there the three of us were in Casey's house at Florida State, holding hands and praying. I said, 'God, please give us strength. I don't know how we're going to do this, but somehow we have to get from Tallahassee to Dunlap and start taking care of things. Please give us strength!'

"By then it was 11 o'clock at night, and it had been a long day for Lisa and me. We had already made the drive from Virginia Beach to Tallahassee that day. Then we had to gather our wits, load up the car, and somehow make a 17-hour drive to Dunlap in a pouring rainstorm."

While driving back to Illinois, the Heths called their middle daughter, Angela, to share the devastating news. Again struck by a detail of memory, Lisa muses, "This all happened on a Saturday night. Angela was at James Madison University and was out most weekend nights. But this particular night, she and her roommate were both in their room."

In Tallahassee, Lisa and Alan packed up Casey as best they could, unsure of how long they'd be in Peoria, and got in their van. Alan remembers, "I absolutely howled for the first hour of the trip. I simply could not stop sobbing. I was driving through the rain and can't even remember much of the drive. It's obvious to me that God was getting us home.

"During the drive we would talk to Angela when we could, but there wasn't a lot of conversation among us. We were each lost in our own thoughts and memories and trying to work out the details of what was ahead."

Family members were locked in their own grief. Lisa says, "I don't even remember much of the 17-hour drive from Tallahassee, but I do remember that it was pouring down rain all the way to the Illinois border."

The closer that the Heths got to Peoria, the more that they knew exactly where they wanted to be: at Northwoods Community Church, surrounded by their church family.

Alan remembers, "My sister lived in Morton, so we stopped there first, and all they wanted to do was love us. The questions began: 'What can we do? How can we help? What do you need?' I said, 'All I really want to do is drop the dogs off here and go to Northwoods.' I didn't mean to hurt their feelings, but we had an overwhelming feeling that we had to get to church.

"People who were gathered at Northwoods had been calling Casey as we got closer to Peoria, so we knew there were a couple hundred of our family's friends waiting for us. I remember pulling up to the church on the circular drive, getting out of the van, and just collapsing into Cal's arms. I was done. I was exhausted and tired, but I was home.

"I don't remember much of what happened then. I know there was a group of people to take care of Lisa and another group of people to take care of Casey. We waited at church for Angela to get home too."

Lisa adds, "When we arrived at Northwoods that Sunday night, it was filled with hundreds of people just waiting to hold us, hug us, and cry with us. People were bringing food and drinks and volunteering to serve and do whatever was necessary. Firehouse Pizza donated several pizzas for the kids to have something to eat. On the day of the funeral, Barrack's Cater Inn provided the meal for both funerals. Their generosity was incredible."

As Alan, Lisa, and Casey waited at Northwoods, surrounded by their church family, Angela made her way back to Peoria to join them. Today, Lisa praises God for the circumstances that fell into place to bring her middle daughter home. She says, "God obviously put Northwoods in our path to prepare us for Ali's death, but He also put a whole lot of other things in our way too.

"My very good friend since childhood had moved to San Diego about 13 years earlier, but at the time of the accident, she was living in Maryland temporarily. That allowed her to be in place to meet our daughter Angela at Dulles Airport in Washington, D.C., and fly to Chicago with her. On top of that, she is a therapist and took care of Angela on the plane.

"My other good friend from childhood was living in Chicago, so she was able to pick them up when they flew in and drive them to Peoria. It's like everyone was in place when they were most needed."

And at Northwoods, seeing Ali and Mary's friends and their overflowing love for the deceased girls was exactly what the Heths needed. Alan remembers, "We came to church and there were literally kids everywhere. That was probably the very best environment I could be in. Even though those kids were all upset and many of them were crying, when I saw them I was reminded of Alison, and that made me feel better somehow.

"We spent the late afternoon and evening at church, and then the reality set in that those kids had to get home and get ready for school and prepare to move on with their lives. We went back to my sister's house in Morton. She had a finished basement and was planning on having us stay there with her, but I couldn't stand the thought of being underground.

"I knew that I had to find someplace in Peoria for us to stay. I didn't know if we would end up with a couple of hotel rooms or an apartment, but I just felt that we had to be near the church because of all the things that had to be done in the coming week or two.

"The thing that probably kept me kind of sane was knowing that there were things that had to be done. I was all about the things that we had to get done. First on my list was finding a place for our family to stay. I decided to call Dale Jorgenson, a realtor friend of mine. I knew Dale worked with a lot of Caterpillar executives and thought that maybe he would have some corporate housing that might be vacant and available for us to rent for a month or two.

"He said he might have an idea of something that could be available. He called me back in a while and said, 'I've got you all taken care of. We've got you in a house that's up for sale right now, and it's only a few blocks from the church.' He had talked to the owner, who told him we were more than welcome to use the house for as long as we wanted.

"It turned out that the homeowner's daughter was a friend of Ali's. It was a huge relief to have a nice place to live, but it didn't even register with me at first that the house was for sale with no one living there, which meant it was empty.

"We finished doing whatever we had to do the night of the visitation and went over to the house, only to find it completely furnished. And I mean completely!"

Lisa elaborates, "It was remarkable. This house went from absolutely vacant to fully furnished in less than 24 hours! There were beds in all the bedrooms, linens, dishes, silverware, toilet paper, Kleenex, a television, food... you name it. People had heard this was where we were going to be living, and they started bringing in ridiculous amounts of food."

Alan explains, "Once Dale found out that the homeowner would let us live in the house, he basically put his entire staff and support personnel on the mission of getting the house ready. He rented furniture and got us a washer and dryer, sheets, towels, laundry detergent... everything. It was an amazing effort!"

The Northwoods church family continued to provide food for the Heths for their entire stay in Peoria, which ended up being about a month long. Alan and Lisa were incredibly thankful for all of the help they received from so many loving neighbors. Most of all, the Heths were grateful for the space that the house provided them to sit and talk with the many friends who reached out to support them in their grief.

"The Monday after Ali's death, we had a lot of things to do, places to go, details to arrange. My good friend Dean Warner was there. He hung around, followed us in his own car when we had to go somewhere because there wasn't room in our car, and helped when we asked. He was just there. It meant a lot, and I haven't forgotten that."

In addition to Dean Warner, the Heths were visited by family, church members, and friends of their own and of Ali's. However, they also received a visit from a seemingly less likely guest.

Alan recounts, "On Monday or Tuesday, a young man named Chris showed up. He was a young guy who lived across the street from us in Virginia Beach. Chris was an interesting young man with a huge heart, but to look at him, you might think differently. He had tattoos everywhere, a buzz haircut, body piercings, a big diamond in one ear, the tilted cap and big baggy clothes.

"I know the first time I saw him in Virginia Beach, my initial thought was, 'Oh great—look who lives across the street!' Then I heard his low-rider truck start up, and I started thinking, 'Oh great! I also get to hear his rumbling truck every day!' But then we got to know him and found out that he was a really nice kid who just had an appearance he wanted to project.

"Chris had gotten to know Casey and Angela when they were at our house, and he of course got to know Ali because she was living with us. He had a pool in his backyard, so all the girls came to know him too. They were all decent friends, but not real close since we hadn't lived there all that long."

In short, Alan and Lisa would certainly not have expected Chris to make the long journey to Peoria for Ali's funeral. But he did. He left the college baseball team he was playing for and made the drive to be with the Heth family. And while he was there, he showed the entire family an outpouring of love.

Lisa explains, "So Chris showed up in Peoria and basically lived on our couch for a week. During that time, he did everything for us. He did our dishes, ran the vacuum cleaner, did errands, and interacted with any younger kids who were visiting us with their parents."

Alan adds, "He's another one of those miracles that happened along the way. You never would have expected him to show up, and yet there he was. I love the kid to this day for the love he showed us."

The Heths stayed in Peoria through the end of March, a little over a month in total. But eventually they knew that the time had come for them to return to Virginia Beach.

Alan says, "One of the things you have to do at some point is try to resume your life and do normal stuff again. You need to go out and celebrate birthdays and the like. I didn't want to go out and Lisa didn't want to go out, but you just have to push yourselves.

"You realize that you have two other daughters and somehow life has to get back on track. You start doing small things. You get up in the morning, you take a shower, you get dressed, and you eat breakfast. You may not feel like doing any of that, but you make yourself do it to try and resume life's routines and rekindle a sense of normalcy."

But in spite of their best efforts, the Heths never felt quite at home in Virginia Beach after that. Alan explains, "I really did try to resume a normal life. I'd get up and try to go about my routine, but in my heart, I knew it wasn't working. I was knocking on doors and going through the motions of trying to sell, but lots had changed. After a while, I told Lisa, 'We have to move back. We've got to go back to Peoria. Your mom is there, my brother and sister are there, and we've got friends there.'

"I'm thinking a lot of my homesickness was from the way our friends, family, and church family had spoiled us with their love after the accident. Everybody was always there for us. When we moved back to Virginia Beach, something had changed in us. We knew where we belonged. We had friends in Virginia and we had fellow believers around us, but we knew where we needed to be.

"It was as plain as the nose on my face. Northwoods was my church home, and I needed it desperately. Lisa and I were supporting each other as much as was humanly possible, but we both needed our family and our friends and our church in our lives if we were going to get through this.

"Parents who go through the loss of a child without Jesus and without friends tell us all we need to know about why the suicide rate is high. I understand why people become addicted and why marriages break up.

"The statistics are incredible. According to the numbers, I should have become a drunk, Lisa and I should have gotten divorced, and one of us should have committed suicide. But with great friends and God's guidance, none of that happened."

Once Alan and Lisa had decided to return to Peoria and their support network, they were still faced with some big questions, such as what to do about Alan's job. He decided to resign from his current company and resume his used medical equipment business.

From there, Alan explains, "So after I had to face the horrible task of telling my best friend and boss that I was quitting his company, we had to sell our house. Admittedly the housing market there was hot at that time, but we sold our house in four hours!

"When we bought our house, I actually saved the 'For Sale by Owner' yard sign. On the Saturday after I'd quit my job, I was out doing yard work, and I popped that sign in the front of the house.

"I put the sign in the yard about 9:30, and at noon a guy and his parents came by and inquired about the house. They toured the inside, and we could see that they really liked it. They kind of huddled up at the end of the driveway, talked for a minute, and then came and told me they wanted to buy it. We got an attorney to handle the details, packed up our stuff, and moved back to Peoria.

"When we got home, our friends Ric and Peg Creasy helped us in another way. They lived in the country outside of Dunlap and had a large metal building in which they allowed us to store our furniture until our house was built. Truly, God took care of all the details for us!"

Settled back in Peoria, the Heths were able to ease into the "new normal" of their lives. Alan found solace in a Bible study with his good friends Dale and Dean. Lisa found herself blessed by the friendship of Sue Salrin, Nancy Tobin, and Laurie Weaver. Both learned to turn to God, and their church, to heal their pain.

Lisa says, "We made the choice to never stop going to church. The first several Sundays were incredibly painful, but we kept pressing on. After Ali died, I knew I had a choice to make. I could be angry and turn from God, or I could be angry and run to Him. And believe me, I was angry!

"I have seen people turn from God, and I knew I didn't want that. I hear Cal say a lot, 'When you don't want to praise Him, do it anyway!'

That was the path I chose to take. It worked for me. I try very hard to surround myself with people who love the Lord as much as I do. We need a support system, and family and friends are necessary.

"It wouldn't have been possible to get where I am today without God. He is my strength, and He gives me peace when I least expect it. A lot of pushing through the pain did not come easily or naturally for me. Much of what I have done in the past six years to get through this has been a conscious choice. I didn't want to drown in my pain, so I chose to live for Jesus."

Alan agrees, saying, "Church is probably one of the things I enjoy most, and one of the things I find most difficult. I am frequently overwhelmed when I am there and am often brought to tears. Thank God it's dark in the auditorium! But it also brings me strength, peace, and joy. I can't imagine my life without it. I thank God for bringing me to Northwoods to prepare me before and help me after Ali's death."

Both Alan and Lisa praise God for bringing them to Northwoods Community Church all those years ago. They are certain that when He brought them both to Christ through Northwoods, He knew what turmoil lay ahead for their family and was laying the foundation for a strong support network in the future.

Alan muses, "Hindsight is 20/20, but I now realize that back in 2001, God had to get my attention, so He put me through some turmoil with my job. At the time, I didn't realize that I was going through my early ordeals with God at my side. Then someone pointed out that I was never alone in my trials. God had to get me going in the right direction, so that I could get our family headed in the right way, so that Ali could be saved before she was killed. In hindsight, it's all so obvious!"

Lisa agrees, saying, "I can't even imagine trying to go through this without Jesus in my life. The lack of hope, the pain and despair would be unbearable. The fact that He prepared us in so many ways beforehand only makes it that much easier."

Alan continues, "God prepared everything in advance so that I could survive. My faith in Jesus has carried me and given me hope. Knowing Alison was a follower of Jesus brings me tremendous comfort! I know I will see her again. That gives me hope! Knowing that Lisa, Casey, and Angela are followers of Jesus gives me comfort in this life and overwhelming joy at the anticipation of our heavenly family reunion!"

The church that brought first Alan, then Lisa, and then their daughter Ali to faith in Christ has also worked with the Heth and Clark families to create a lasting memento to the teenagers' faith. Lisa explains, "After the funeral and things had settled down, we asked the church if we could plant a tree in Alison's memory. They not only let us plant several trees, but also allowed us to build a double gazebo on the property next to the lake in memory of Ali and Mary. I feel so incredibly blessed to be part of this church."

In turn, the Heths try to give back some of what they have received. Alan says, "Serving others is also a great blessing. I coach girls' basketball, due in large part to Pat Garst (Dunlap High School varsity girls basketball coach), who gave me an opportunity when I needed it most. It's very hard for me sometimes because I spent most of Ali's childhood coaching her in basketball. I see her every time I step into the gym, but the time I spend with the girls is so rewarding."

To those who have never experienced the loss of a loved one, Alan says, "Don't take your children for granted. They might not always be there. Love them, hug them, discipline them, lead them, and spend as much time with them as you can! Talk to them, have dinner with them, take them on vacation. Just spend time with them. Life can sometimes get in the way, but do your best to be with them. They need you, and they are a good investment of your time and energy. They will pay dividends many times over."

To those who have suffered losses similar to their own, Lisa advises, "Don't give up on God. It's okay to be mad. He understands. He will be there for you. Stay close to your church family and surround yourself with those who love the Lord. And although I fought it for a long time, I think it is very important to get some sort of counseling. I am not comfortable in a group, so I chose one-on-one. I won't lie and say it is easy. It's not. It's incredibly painful at times, but it is so important to work through your grief."

Alan confirms this, saying, "My advice would be 'Lean in!' Lean into Jesus, your Bible, your family, your friends, and the church... and get counseling. I resisted counseling, but then realized if I did it, Lisa and the girls might also."

So today, over six years after their daughter Alison's death, Alan and Lisa Heth are taking their own advice, still "leaning in" to the loving arms of their Northwoods' family. Alan says, "I love Northwoods Community Church. The people are so supportive. God's love through these people has helped with our load. Whenever my grief gets too heavy to carry, God sends someone to help carry it for a while."

And most importantly, Alan and Lisa never forget that they are forever bonded to their daughter in the Lord.

Lisa says, "Every day that goes by, we miss Ali more and more. But it's also one more day closer to seeing her again. And I *will* see her again."

Alan concludes, "It may be a little selfish, but I can't wait until the day when I see her in Heaven and she runs up and throws her arms around me and hugs me again. And as I look over her shoulder, I'll see Jesus. What a day that will be!"

As long as I live, I will never forget the sorrow and pain surrounding Ali and Mary's deaths. I had been scheduled to fly to Tucson, Arizona, following our worship services that weekend to meet up with some of my family for a little fun at my brother's ranch.

Instead, for the next few days, I found myself walking through every pastor's nightmare. I re-scheduled my flight for later in the week and thus it was, a few days later with the funerals over and completely exhausted, I drove to Chicago to catch a flight to Tucson. It was during that drive that God ministered to my heart through a Southern Gospel song (it's no secret I'm a Southern Gospel quartet nut), which I played over and over again the whole way to Chicago.

The words of the chorus said, "God is still good when the waves roll high. God is still good all through the night. When I've done all I can and I don't understand, God is still good. Clouds of doubt may darken my way, but showers of blessing will come any day; He'll bring me through and I'll stand and say, 'God is still good.'"

I must have sobbed and cried my way through that song no less than 50 times on my way to Chicago. And each time I did, I would be praying in my spirit, "God, I'm claiming this for Alan and Lisa. Oh God, let your power and grace overshadow them such that on the other side of this devastating loss, they'll still be standing and proclaiming, 'God is still good.'"

Six years later, this chapter is the answer to that prayer.

Back On
Her Feet

Vicky's Story

> *"Almost like a broken bone that needs to be reset, God
> breaks us where we need to be broken. He fractures the
> pride and lust and anger in our lives, but He does it to
> remodel us in His image. And once we heal, we end
> up stronger than we were to begin with."*
>
> IN A PIT WITH A LION ON A SNOWY DAY BY MARK BATTERSON

I still remember the moment like it was yesterday. I was 15
years old and in my sophomore year of high school basketball. I was
nursing a sprained arch in my foot, and the injury had severely limited
my ability to jump. One of the big reasons I loved to play basketball
was because I loved to jump. But now I was grounded.

As I went to bed one night, I asked Jesus to heal my foot. From
all the accounts I had read in the New Testament, it seemed to me that

Jesus was pretty willing to heal people who came to Him with their hurts and diseases. I can't say that I expected Him to heal me, but in my simple faith, it only seemed right to ask Him.

The next morning when I woke up, I was getting ready to step out of bed when I reminded myself, "Be careful not to put too much pressure on your right foot." But when I stepped down on it, I could tell that something was different. I pushed a little harder and no pain. Again, I pushed even harder and still no pain. After three or four tests the giddy reality began to break in on my mind: "I think Jesus healed my foot." Subsequent pain-free practices proved that He had indeed answered my prayer. In fact, I've had no problems with my arch from that moment forward.

As thrilling as that miracle moment was in my life, nothing was to compare to the joy of discovering years later that God really can, and often does, heal our hurts and diseases. While the mystery of unanswered prayer will never be solved this side of heaven, over the years I have seen God's healing power released in people's lives often enough that I have made it a conscious practice in my life, and in the life of our church, to pray for God's healing in people's lives. And always I am amazed at His goodness and love when He steps in to heal in a tangible way.

One lady who experienced God's healing touch in an amazing way was Vicky Johnson. I well remember the night we prayed for her, asking God to heal both her broken heart and her boot-clad broken foot. You can imagine my shock when only three days later, I walked into the church for our Saturday night service and found Vicky, walking around in shoes, serving at our Connections café.

I said to her in shocked disbelief, "What are you doing?" She looked at me with eyes beaming and responded, "God healed me instantly on Wednesday night. My foot has been fine since then and not only that, but He touched my heart as well." Amazing! Let her story serve to increase your faith in the fact that God can heal your hurts.

To celebrate the arrival of her 40th birthday, Vicky Johnson decided to prove to her 14-year-old son that she was still young, active, and fun. Vicky was certain that she could still rollerblade, so she told her son to grab his skateboard and go on a sidewalk adventure with his mother.

After a slow start, Vicky felt like she had regained her teenage form. She does admit, however, that trying to jump a curb may not have been her best birthday idea, as it earned her a trip to the emergency room. The result was a lot of scrapes, a broken foot, and a damper on her birthday celebration.

Little did Vicky know that this was just the beginning of an odyssey which would continue for the next six months.

She remembers, "I went to the hospital, and sure enough, it was broken. I went to a specialist, and he put me in a cast and a walking boot. After about four weeks, I noticed that my leg would turn purple. During this whole ordeal, it burned like it was on fire.

"I went back to the doctor, and he diagnosed me with RSDS, which stands for Reflex Sympathetic Dystrophy Syndrome. It's an ailment where your body's nerve endings know something is going on and become confused. Their way of reacting is to become inflamed.

"My specialist explained that doctors don't really have a cure for RSDS or even agree on what makes it happen. It almost always occurs in a traumatized part of your body. He put me on an anti-inflammatory drug and nerve pain medicine. The RSDS seemed to temporarily get better.

"I broke my foot in May, and by September, the bone was still not healing correctly. There was pain 24 hours a day and it was a real nuisance. I'm an active person and God brought me to a standstill.

"Meanwhile, the whole time this was going on, my 24-year-old sister Rachel was in a very, very dark place in her life. There are three sisters in my family, and we had always been very close. We were raised in a Christian home, and Rachel especially was always the kind of girl who never gave Mom and Dad even a moment of problems. As my baby sister, Rachel was the light of my life. She loved the Lord from the time she was a little girl and was always just the perfect child.

"She took a new job and moved to a new city in 2006, and there she met a guy who got her in a trap of control and manipulation. From 2006 to 2008, Rachel really pulled away from my other sister Tonya and me. It was a horrible, horrible time. We went from being super, super close to not even talking for six months. Seeing her willful rebellion against God and family was incredibly painful.

"At the same time, my foot wasn't healing normally. I went to the doctor, and he had to go back in and take out some bone and scrape off some other areas. After this surgery, the bone started healing properly, but the RSDS got worse. At this point, I was in constant pain. The medication didn't help at all."

$$\cdots\prec\!\infty\!\succ\cdots$$

"One Wednesday night, a month after my second surgery, I went to Northwoods even though it hurt so badly that I didn't even want to leave the house. I just wanted to stay home and feel sorry for myself. I'm guessing I was in a depressed state by that time. I was dealing with the physical situation and the problem with my sister, but I kept reminding myself that my best hope was to trust God.

"On that particular Wednesday, my middle sister Tonya and I were going to go to church and then go see a movie afterward. We got to church and I changed my mind and said, 'Tonya, let's just go to the movie theatre.' So we drove there and Tonya was going to drop me off at the door. Suddenly I said, 'I can't do this. We need to go to church!' She pleaded with me to just make up my mind, and again I told her I knew that we needed to be at church.

"We went in and sat in the back. There was an awesome message being preached, but my leg was so inflamed and I was in so much pain that it was hard to stay focused. At the end, the pastor called for anyone needing prayer to come forward. I knew I needed to go up front for prayer for my leg, but I was in too much pain to walk up there.

"At that time, Tonya was separated from her husband and struggling with her own issues. Having been through a divorce five years earlier, I really sympathized with what she was going through. So Tonya went forward because she wanted prayer to give her the strength and wisdom to do the right thing as a wife and mother.

"I try to never be a complainer, so Tonya didn't really understand the level of pain I was suffering. I'm sitting in the back watching these people be prayed over and silently saying, 'I need to be prayed over, God. I'm going to trust You, Lord. I know that you know what I need and will provide it in Your time.'

"I left the auditorium and wandered into the bookstore, wanting so much to have someone pray over me. The first person I saw walking by was Cal Rychener. I immediately thought maybe I could catch up with Cal and ask him to pray for me. I couldn't walk fast enough to catch him. It looked like Cal was on a mission, going somewhere else, and I could hardly hobble.

"I stopped where I was and just closed my eyes and prayed, 'God, right now I need to know that You are there. Please bring someone here to pray for me. I can't walk now, Lord, so You're going to have to bring someone to me.'

"I opened my eyes and Cal was standing right in front of me, saying, 'What happened?'

"I told him that he wouldn't believe all that was going on, but I asked him just to pray for me and my RSDS.

"He asked me to go over to a couch and have a seat while he went to get Leesa Tiethoff. Leesa heads up the Northwoods prayer ministry. They asked me what was going on, and I explained that I had quit taking the prescribed medication four days earlier because it wasn't doing me any good. I told them how I could hardly function because of the pain.

"They were praying over me, but all of a sudden Leesa stopped and said, 'I feel like there is something going on in your heart that is affecting the healing in your foot and your leg.'

"I told her about Tonya's separation from her husband and that it was dredging up memories of my own divorce. I told her that Tonya's pain was heavy on my heart. Leesa prayed for that situation, and since she is a wife and a mother, she really connected with Tonya's ordeal.

"She stopped again and quoted Ephesians 6 where it talks about how our feet are shod with the peace of Jesus and that's what we're to carry into the world. She said she felt like there was something deeper going on in my heart."

"I may not have known the depths of the hurt that my separation from my baby sister had created. I remember coming out of my surgery, where I really had no control over what I was going to feel or say. I immediately started heaving with sobs. That moment praying with

Leesa and Cal was the same sensation, where I was just overcome with grief for my sister.

"At first I was really guarded, but Leesa listened to the Spirit of God and knew there was something deeper I wasn't saying. She finally convinced me to share when she said, 'There is something going on that is affecting your ability to carry the peace of Jesus with your feet.'

"It was then that I told her that my little sister was running 100 miles an hour in the wrong direction. I told her Rachel was running away from God and was caught in a rebellion and didn't know how to get out.

"As soon as I told Leesa this, I felt this amazing burden being lifted. She just started praying in the Spirit of the Lord over me and laying hands on me. I remember her praying that God would protect Rachel and bring her back to Himself. It was never our family's prayer that God would bring my sister back to us. Our prayer was always, 'God, bring her back to You. Please open her eyes and open her heart.'

"I always knew that if she was right with God, then she would be right with her whole family.

"So Leesa was praying and Cal was praying. She laid her hands on my leg from my knee down to my foot where all the pain had been concentrated. As they were praying, I literally felt the burning sensation turn into this soothing tingle. I know some people think I'm crazy, but it literally was like I could feel the hand of Jesus on me.

"To that point, I had experienced constant pain in that leg for nearly four months. It was 24 hours a day, seven days a week. As hard as it is to imagine, I was healed instantly. Like most Christians, I've prayed for healing in others, but when it actually happened to me, it was just so intense and so immediate.

"Meanwhile, my sister Tonya hadn't seen me since she had gone up to the front of the church to ask for prayers for her situation. At some point, she had gone to get the car so I wouldn't have to hobble to the parking lot. The whole time, which was probably about 20 minutes, Tonya was sitting out in front waiting for me to come out.

"I literally went to the car as normal as ever. As I look back on that moment of instantaneous healing, I think I should have been jumping up and down!

"So I got in the car and said, 'Tonya, you're not going to believe what just happened!' While I'm saying this, I'm ripping the boot off my foot. My sister is kind of conservative and low-key. She was probably thinking I had completely lost it.

"But I explained everything that had happened and that the pain and burning were gone. I only live a couple of miles from Northwoods, but we were quite literally praising Jesus during the drive home!"

————••◆••————

"After I had been home for about an hour, I knew it was real. I had gone a full hour without pain and I was jumping up and down. Tonya was happy for me, but also saying, 'Let's just take it easy here, Vicky. Don't go over the top and re-injure yourself.'

"I was saying, 'Jesus healed me! I feel like the paralytic who picked up his mat and went on his way!' That night I went to bed without elevating my leg or taking any precautions, and I slept perfectly for the first time in four months. I remember waking up the next morning with the sun pouring in my windows, and I had this huge smile on my face.

"It was all just so *real*. It's important to grasp that not only did God heal the RSDS in my foot, but he also healed my heart. As I look back, I think that's what I was so elated about. I really felt like He had taken that burden of Rachel completely off of me. No longer did I feel like it was necessary for me to fix it.

"I felt like I had been depending on God for the year and a half before this incident. I had never prayed like that before. I was on my face constantly. I was in His Word constantly. I would close myself off in my bedroom for alone time with God. I felt like I was doing everything I could, but I realize now that I was still trying to carry it myself. I had let the hurt and worry over my sister go so deep into my heart that it was affecting everything.

"After all of this, I went back to my doctor. He had an MRI done, and it didn't even show a break. There was no evidence of my foot ever having been broken. In the intervening years, the RSDS has never returned.

"My doctor, who was a Hindu from India, couldn't explain the healing other than to say, 'We don't understand the onset of RSDS, and it can leave as fast as it comes.'

"That may well be true, but the odds of such a coincidence when people are praying and laying hands on me is just too high to calculate.

"An important lesson from all of this for me is that our feet are to carry the peace of Jesus. It really doesn't matter what the situation is. As Christ-followers, that's what we are supposed to do."

Through her experiences that Wednesday night at Northwoods, Vicky Johnson has to irrevocably believe in the healing power of prayer. In addition to her own physical healing, God also heard and answered her family's other prayers that night. Within three months of that night, Tonya and her husband sought Christian counsel and recommitted their marriage, and Rachel found the strength to leave her abusive boyfriend and reunite herself with her loving family. Rachel has told

Vicky that even when she was in the darkest of places, she could feel her sisters' love and prayers.

Vicky says, "Looking back, I think now that it took me some time to understand the whole impact of that night of healing prayer. God is so big that I don't think our small minds can comprehend the vastness of His power... how He can touch us and heal us through the hands of humans."

Friend, I don't know what hurts and pains you may be carrying in your own life these days, but I hope you will open your heart to the possibility and reality that God can and does heal today. No, not always and certainly not always on our timetable. But isn't it worth asking Him? Isn't it worth seeking Him? Isn't it worth knocking on the door of heaven and finding, as He promised, grace and mercy to help us in our time of need? What have you got to lose? You may just find yourself amazed at what God can do when you place your hurts in His hands.

(The names in this narrative have been changed at the request of the characters.)

Up Out of the Trenches

Mark & Amy's Story

*"Dear brothers and sisters, when troubles come your way,
consider it an opportunity for great joy. For you know that
when your faith is tested, your endurance has a chance to grow."*

JAMES 1:2-3

Author Philip Yancey has wisely stated that life seems to offer us two alternatives: disappointment with God or disappointment without Him. Either way, life offers none of us the guarantee of a disappointment-free existence. It's when the tribulations and trials of life strike close to home that a crisis of faith is often not far behind. For some, it seems that life's trials serve only to harden their hearts and drive them away from God.

I think of a situation a number of years ago with a young man in his early thirties who told me that he was an atheist. I inquired as to how he had come to the conclusion that God did not exist when it seems that there is abundant evidence to the contrary. He said to me, "My dad died of cancer when he was in his early 60's. All of our prayers for God to save his life and heal him did nothing to stave off death. I can't believe that a loving God, if He were really there, would have allowed my father to die. So I have concluded that He doesn't exist."

However, others encounter trouble and turmoil in life and end up turning to God in the midst of their pain and confusion. Such was the case for Mark and Amy Vonachen, whose life circumstances brought them to their knees. However, from that position they turned into worshipers of the God who has today raised them to their feet and enabled them to overcome in spite of their hardships. They are a reminder that no matter what life has thrown at you, our God can restore and bring healing to our deepest disappointments.

Mark and Amy Vonachen's marriage was plagued by troubles from the very first day of their union.

Amy was already pregnant when they got married in January of 1995. But on the morning after their wedding, she miscarried their child.

With 16 years' perspective on this sad event, Mark can now say, "As I look back, I see God saying to us, 'The miscarriage was a horrible event, but now you are together in marriage, and that's where I want you to be.'"

As the years continued, Mark and Amy experienced two more miscarriages together. However, they were ultimately blessed with three beautiful, healthy children. Druschel was born in November of that year and Jabe was born the following January, a mere 13+ months apart.

The young family faced another tragedy on New Year's Day of 1999. Amy's mother, father, and 7-year-old niece were caught in a house fire. The neighbor who reported the fire to 9-1-1 called the Vonachens right away, and since they lived less than five minutes away from Amy's parents, they arrived on the scene shortly after the fire department.

Mark remembers, "As we arrived, we saw Amy's father lying in the middle of the street. No sheet covering him, no EMTs working on him, just lying there. Amy came running to me in a panic as we then witnessed the firemen carrying her mother from the house. The firemen had already pulled Amy's niece from the house too, and they were working on her in the back of the ambulance. It turned out that all three of them had actually died prior to being taken from the house."

In the months that followed, Amy went through an incredible amount of turmoil. Mark regretfully remembers, "Not only did she have to handle her emotions, but she was also left with the task of handling her parents' estate, rebuilding her childhood home, burying her parents and niece, and taking care of our two young children. The finances and the insurance claims and the rebuilding of the house all fell upon her. As her husband, I was trying very hard to support her, but I was lost and chose to run the other direction. It was a hard time for our family and marriage.

"We still talk about that time in our lives today. With all of the things she was handling, Amy had lots of questions about her parents' death, and I wasn't able to give her the right answers. I wanted her to lean on me for support, but I only had a limited knowledge of the things that needed to be done. It was very frustrating for both of us.

"Our family was suffering during that time. There were a lot of emotions in our home. I don't know that we were thinking of divorce at that time, but our lives were clearly crazy. We had the normal parental responsibilities. Amy was a stay-at-home mother of our two young children, I was working a lot of hours as the Director of Operations for the Peoria Chiefs baseball team plus my summer obligation to the National Guard, and Amy had mounds of responsibilities relating to the fire and her parents' deaths. I think she was suffering from post-traumatic stress. Then we found out that Amy was pregnant with our third child. This only added to the stress that our marriage and family were already under.

"We were suffering as individuals, as a couple, and as a family. At that point, I sought help from a counselor and psychiatrist. I tried to get Amy to go too, but she never would. I think she didn't want to have to relive her story and her memories. At that point, she hadn't really dealt with all her feelings and emotions from losing her parents and niece in the fire. I think that time in our lives shaped the tone of our marriage for quite a while."

In spite of their suffering, the Vonachens tried to move forward with their lives. In December of 2000, their third child, Jac, was born. At that time, Amy was a stay-at-home mom and occasionally substitute taught in Peoria's District 150 to utilize her college degree in education. But in 2002, she embarked on a completely new professional endeavor. She was hired as the Director of Business Development at a logistics firm headquartered in Danville, Illinois, which necessitated a move for the young family.

Through Amy, Mark got to know her boss, who liked what Mark had done with the Peoria Chiefs and how he had run the facility there. Shortly afterwards, Mark was brought onboard as the Director of Operations for the growing logistics company.

But before they had time to fully adjust to their new roles or their new home, another change rocked their household. Mark remembers, "We had moved to Danville, and after about six months on the job, my National Guard unit got activated and I had to report for duty in Iraq.

"I had to leave Amy in Danville with three young kids, a new home, and a new job as an executive in a new company. It was a lot for her to handle. About the only support she had was from a small church we had started attending.

"We hadn't been going to church at all before, but we found this small, non-denominational church that our boss was attending. He talked us into trying it out and Amy and I started going regularly."

Though Mark had attended church regularly as a child, his church attendance as an adult was usually tied to holidays and special times with his parents. However, this small church in Danville was to become a refuge for the Vonachens.

In November of 2003, Mark left Amy to the support of their small church in Danville and departed to serve within the structure of the National Guard. This was still very early on in the war; Mark's unit was brought in to replace the first wave of soldiers who had been sent over.

He says, "Of the 15 months I was gone, a year of it was spent in Iraq. That was a really rough time for Amy. When I was in Iraq, that was maybe the first time that I got a strong feeling that my marriage needed to change. I truly missed my family. Prior to my deployment in Iraq, I probably could have gone away for a weekend and not missed my family life because it was always so hectic.

"I was thrown into a different world when I went to Iraq. I was a helicopter crew chief on Blackhawk helicopters. One of the jobs attached to that position is that of a gunner, so I flew all the time in less than ideal conditions. By the end of my time there, I had over 630 combat flight hours.

"The mortality rate isn't the best for that job. We lost three aircraft from our battalion while it was positioned in Iraq. Two of the aircraft were shot down — one Chinook, just before we arrived in country, was hit by a SAM (Surface-to-Air Missile) and one Blackhawk from small arms and RPG (Rocket Propelled Grenade) while I was there. I was always worried something would happen to me and that my wife would be left trying to raise three kids and asking so many questions.

"I flew almost every day over Baghdad, or Fallujah, or Mosul, or some other place. I didn't see heavy combat, but the strain of going out on a mission every day and not knowing if or when you would be shot at is something that takes a psychological toll. Our base was in a place called 'Mortar Alley', and we were mortared every day.

"We flew no higher than 50 feet and at a speed of 145 knots wherever we went. I saw a lot of things I won't forget. I have hauled body bags and done casualty evacuations. Things like that leave a lasting impression."

------··◄∞►··------

"I volunteered for so many missions because I believed that's why I was over there. Some guys would come up with any excuse not to fly, but I felt it was my duty. I was a soldier, and that's why I was there. I always had a sense of watching my buddies' backs. I wanted to be with them because I had the feeling that if I were on their mission, nothing bad would happen to them.

"We formed lots of bonds in our crew. In many ways, we were inseparable. My best friend in the Guard was a guy from Decatur, Illinois. He was a Christian, so his faith was right under my nose, but I still didn't get it. During my year in Iraq, I went to one religious service. That was Christmas 2004. My friend would listen to Christian music and read the Bible, but I don't think he ever imagined that I would have listened to it if he had tried to talk to me about Jesus.

"By the time I was deployed in Iraq, I had been in the Guard for 18 years. I had been through hours and hours of training. When you're being trained, you question why you're doing the same thing over and over again. But when you get in combat, all the things you've learned during training just kick in automatically. You don't even have to think about how to react. Instinct takes over and you respond to a situation properly.

"The strange thing about all of this is that I enjoyed doing it. It makes me think about the book *Wild at Heart*. In that book, John Eldredge tells of someone whose boat was caught in a hurricane in the middle of the ocean. The boat capsized and he says, 'It was the best time of my life.'

"When I first read that, I said, 'Wow! That is so true!' I think it's because during a combat mission, all of your senses are heightened and you do feel very alert and alive."

But while the stress of serving on combat missions in Iraq could make Mark feel invigorated at times, the everyday stress of holding together the home front had a different effect on Amy.

Mark remembers, "Because of the stress she was facing, Amy lost her job during the last month that I was in Iraq. This was particularly hard on us because she was fired from the same company that I eventually had to come back and work at.

"Before you come home, the military puts you through a lot of briefings where they tell you that things won't be the same at home as when you left. They warn you that returning to normal life will take time.

"What might have been a fairly smooth transition got all jumbled up because of our jobs. I was going back to work for the small company that had fired Amy, and that wasn't easy. The company had changed in the time I was gone, and on top of that, my wife was pretty stressed."

Part of Amy's stress was some news that Mark's family had been keeping from him while he was serving in the National Guard. Mark remembers, "Within three days of my coming home, my brother-in-law, George Shadid Jr., passed away. He had been diagnosed as having a brain tumor prior to my leaving for Iraq, but nobody had told me how poorly he was doing because they didn't want to worry me. Amy kept telling my family to let me know the truth about George, but they didn't want me to have any more things to worry about.

"When I got back to the States, they told me we needed to come to Peoria and see George because he wasn't doing too well. I walked in to find him in bed but largely incoherent. To say the least, I was unprepared for the state that I saw George in. He died that same evening.

"I felt like I came home from a war, hit the ground running, and haven't slowed down since. That's something I battle every day. I went back to work 10 days after returning to the States and was expected to be as normal as if I had been gone for a long weekend."

But Mark wasn't his old version of "normal." After all that he had seen and been through, dealing with everyday life was much more of a challenge. He says, "I came back from Iraq with Post-Traumatic Stress Disorder. I tried to seek help through the Veterans Administration, but it didn't help. At that time, when the war was still young, the V.A. was not prepared for the problems of returning soldiers. Their idea of treatment was to give you medication, talk about it a little bit, and shove you out the door.

"If all of that wasn't enough, my mom was also battling cancer at that time. So with everything that was going on with my family and our jobs, we made the decision to move back to Peoria.

"The post-traumatic stress got worse and worse. I'd hear noises and about hit the floor, or I would get a feeling of hyper-vigilance. Sudden loud noises were horrible for me. Sometimes I would wish I was still there flying missions. I'm a lot better today, but I can still have an occasional feeling if I come across a smell, noise, or sight that reminds me of Iraq.

"I had an incident not too long ago at Sam's Club. I was sitting on a bench at the café. I looked up and they had a plywood wall covering up the area where they were doing some remodeling. Something as simple as that plywood wall triggered memories of when I was in Kuwait. We used to stay in these warehouses that had plywood walls, and seeing that wall at Sam's gave me the feeling of being in Kuwait again. I got a rush and a pounding in my chest just from its sight and smell. It was a feeling of separation and not being able to come home for a long time."

When the Vonachen family moved back to Peoria, Mark says, "I was able to get a job with the Department of Defense working on Chinook helicopters at the National Guard base. We bought a house in Dunlap. But just as things started to settle down, I was called up by the Guard for a month of active duty in relation to Hurricane Katrina."

After another month of separation from his family, Mark returned to Peoria and his job with the Department of Defense. One day while he was at work, one of the pilots he had flown with in Iraq came in and told him about a job opening that involved working on medevac helicopters at a local hospital. The pilot told Mark that they needed a mechanic and encouraged him to apply.

Mark says, "I got my civilian license and applied for the medevac job. I got the job and started working there part-time in early 2006, then began full-time work in August of 2006. But during that whole time, our marriage wasn't going well. We were growing apart.

"The helicopter medevac department is an entity off by itself and is largely separate from the hospital. It was really not a very good environment for me. You have doctors and nurses and pilots and a mixture of all Type A personalities thrown together. I got drawn into that environment and away from my family and my wife.

"After I had been there about six months, everything was just spinning. My mom's condition had gotten worse, and my relationship with my wife and kids felt very distant. That's where my life just fell off the cliff. Not only was I dealing with post-traumatic stress, anxiety and depression, but also now the loss of my mom and the potential loss of my family came into play.

"I would come home from work so down and depressed that I would sit on the couch and stare at the walls all evening. I wished I could just dig a deep hole and climb in. I wasn't doing anything with the kids or with Amy. I just had no energy and no interest in anything. It didn't matter what Amy would say to me. I just couldn't find the purpose for my life."

By 2007, Mark was a complete mess. He loved Amy and their three children, but his post-traumatic stress and depression made it hard for him to interact with them. His job increased his anxiety, and he felt that he was spinning without purpose. He didn't want to burden his family with all of his troubles.

He says, "Amy and I had tried marriage counseling, but each time we went, we would come away worse off than ever. It always seemed that the counselor would do nothing more than stir up lots of emotions.

"In the summer of 2007, I tried leaving Amy several times. I would pack my bags and leave a note behind, trying to explain myself to her. I hoped she would understand what I was going through. But Amy always convinced me to come back.

"The thought of Amy being alone kept me in our marriage more than once. Three times that summer I tried to walk out, but each time I thought that our marriage was over, something brought me back. One time I managed to escape for a week without talking to Amy about any of it. I just e-mailed her.

"Amy told me this was when she started to pray. Sometimes she would pray for hours. While I was at work and the kids were at school, she would listen to Christian music and pray until I returned from work. I was amazed to find out later that she had been praying for our marriage.

"Another time after I attempted to leave, my sister came and got me. She took me to my brother's house. Two of my brothers and my sister were there. They sat me down and tried to get me to tell them what was really going on.

"My brother Dan is an elder at Grace Presbyterian Church in Peoria. He kept saying, 'I don't think this is a marriage thing or a post-traumatic stress issue either. This is a spiritual issue. Mark doesn't need counseling. He is in the midst of spiritual warfare.'

"My brother told me that he would make a commitment to help me get through my ordeal. Then he told me he had someone in mind that he wanted me to see. He said the man was a Bible-based counselor.

"I went to see this Christian counselor thinking, 'Great, here I go again. I'm going to have to tell someone new my whole story. He'll want to know why I'm here and I'll have to go through it all again.'

"I went into my story about how I felt and what happened to me in Iraq and all the anxiety I was dealing with. After I was done, the counselor pulled out his Bible and read me James 1:2-3 about trials and tribulations.

"Then he went into other Biblical verses and actually explained to me what I was feeling and why it was happening to me. I started to break down. I was crying and saying, 'I don't know what's going on here.'

"I couldn't explain anything that was happening. Everything he said to me was straight from the Bible. It was all right there. I'd always had a Bible. I flew with one in my helmet bag. But having a Bible with you in combat and not reading it makes it nothing more than a lucky rabbit's foot.

"The bottom line is that I didn't have a relationship with the Lord. It was September 18, 2008, and I accepted Christ into my life that day. From that day on, things really started changing in my marriage. That's when I started reading the Bible and applying what I read to my life.

"When I stopped for a moment and really thought about it, I realized how awful I felt. I knew in my heart that I could not leave Amy and our kids.

"Shortly after I had accepted Christ in my life, Amy went to see my counselor and she also accepted Christ."

Mark continues, "I hadn't been to church and gotten anything out of it in years, but God had given me so many signs! Northwoods Community Church was across from the entrance to our neighborhood. I would see it every time I left or came home. I saw thousands of people file in there on Sundays and I often wondered what was going on in there... what those people knew that I didn't.

"The weekend after we accepted Christ, Amy and I decided to check out Northwoods for the first time. We checked our kids in to the children's Sunday School programs and then we entered the auditorium. The message was great, but the thing that really captured my heart and soul was the worship music. It was loud and intense. When we stood for worship to start the service, I was absorbed. I started crying and just couldn't stop. Amy and I were holding hands and crying. We continued to cry every service after that for a month or two. We could not wait to go back, so we could get the same feelings all over again.

"That first day, and every time since, when I come into the auditorium, it's like I'm entering a bomb shelter. Everything that has been bombarding me all week long is put on hold. I can feel the Holy Spirit has come over me. I get a tingle that I can feel throughout my body. When I pray, I always know that God is present and that He is listening to me.

"As I started my new walk with Northwoods, I could see myself changing. I started reading the Bible, coming to church every week, leading my family in the right direction, and meeting lots of positive people. Next I began to participate in the men's group and take classes that the church offered. The first class I took was titled *When the Joy Is Gone*. That's when it hit me that I wasn't alone.

"When I attended the men's group, it was like God brought this group of men together just for me! It was like He had handpicked these men to help me on my spiritual journey. These men shared the facts about what they had gone through or what they were going through. Many were facing the same trials I had been going through. Some had been in affairs. Some had been alcoholics or drug addicts. Some had known war in Vietnam or Iraq, and some had felt anxiety and depression. I realized then that I wasn't alone. I had people around who wanted to help me. I found myself with some close and important friendships.

"If I hadn't found Northwoods, I don't know where I would be today. I think it's safe to say I wouldn't be with Amy and my children. I know I would have continued on a destructive path. God, along with the patient and forgiving attitude of my wife, coupled with the support of my brother Dan, and my men's group, have changed my life.

"I learned a lot about spiritual warfare when I first accepted Jesus. I'm a firm believer that Satan didn't want me to be happy and he didn't want me to be married.

"God brought Amy and me together through marriage. Knowing all and seeing that our marriage was not going to withstand everything that was being thrown at us, He chose a different way to keep us together."

Through all of the pain and struggles that the Vonachens have faced over the past 16 years, even from the first day of their marriage, God has kept them together. Even when Mark gave up hope and tried to leave, God restored their family. And when Mark and Amy placed their faith in Him, He brought them up out of the trenches.

I ran into Mark and Amy just shortly after I had been working on this chapter for the book and I said to them, "Guys, I'm not sure how you're even standing today in light of what you've been through. Your lives are a testimony to the power of God to bring us through our most difficult struggles because there is no other explanation for why you didn't just crumble under the weight of your life circumstances."

To anyone who may be walking through a fiery trial at this very moment, I would remind you of God's promise in 1 Peter 5:10, "And the God of all grace, who had called you to His eternal glory in Christ, after you have suffered for a little while, will Himself restore you and make you strong, firm, and steadfast."

This verse simply means that what God brings you to, He will bring you through. Draw near to Him, trust Him, continue to worship and obey Him, and He will bring you up out of the trenches.

Together...
For Better Or Worse

Glen & Shelly's Story

"True obedience to God means doing what He says, when He says, how He says, as long as He says, until what He says is accomplished. Unfortunately this concept is often rejected in today's culture."

LIVING THE EXTRAORDINARY LIFE BY CHARLES F. STANLEY

There's no question that marriages are under attack like never before. And it should not surprise us that our enemy takes particular delight in targeting the one relationship on earth that God intended to be an illustration of the kind of affectionate love that Jesus Christ has for His bride, the Church (see Ephesians 5:22-33). If our children want a picture of what Jesus Christ's love for us is like, they shouldn't have to look any further than simply watching their dad love their mom. If they want a picture of how we should respond to Christ's love for us, they shouldn't have to look any further than watching their mom love their dad. So what kind of picture are our children getting from the marriages they are observing in our homes?

A few years ago, the students at Columbia Bible College were given a picture they wouldn't soon forget when their president, Robert McQuilken, announced his resignation in one of their chapels. He was leaving so he could care for his wife, Muriel, who was suffering from the advanced stages of Alzheimer's disease. In McQuilken's resignation letter he wrote:

"My dear wife, Muriel, has been in failing mental health for about eight years. So far I have been able to carry both her ever-growing needs and my leadership responsibilities at CBC. But recently it has become apparent that Muriel is contented most of the time she is with me and almost none of the time I am away from her. It is not just 'discontent.' She is filled with fear — even terror — that she has lost me and always goes in search for me when I leave home. So it is clear to me that she needs me now, full-time.

"Perhaps it would help you to understand if I shared with you what I shared at the time of my resignation in chapel. The decision was made, in a way, 42 years ago when I promised to care for Muriel 'in sickness and in health... 'til death do us part.' So, as I told the students and faculty, as a man of my word, integrity has something to do with it. But so does fairness. She has cared for me fully and sacrificially all these years; if I cared for her the next 40 years I would not be out of debt. Duty, however, can be grim and stoic.

"But there is more; I love Muriel. She is a delight to me – her childlike dependence and confidence in me, her warm love, occasional flashes of wit I used to relish so, her happy spirit and tough resilience in the face of her continual distressing frustration. I do not have to care for her, I get to! It is a high honor to care for so wonderful a person."

What a powerful picture of the kind of covenantal love God wants us to demonstrate in our marriages! And if that picture has gotten lost or distorted or broken in your marriage, I want you to know that our God can pick up the broken pieces of a marriage gone bad and paint a whole new picture of what He had in mind. It's just a matter of whether He can find a couple of willing partners who will humble themselves and obey whatever He says... like Glen and Shelly Penning.

••◄◯◯►••

Their story began in 1978. Twelve-year-old Shelly Farson asked God to show her who her future husband would be. Shortly afterwards, she saw Glen Penning. They began dating when they were 13 years old. The rest, as they say, is history.

Glen and Shelly married in 1985, when they were 20 years old. By the time they were 28, the Pennings had three sons. They had been together for 15 years, more than half of their lives. Yet they were both convinced that their marriage was about to end.

Glen remembers, "I was working for the city of Pekin, going to school, and trying to do everything that young dads do to create a good life for their family. Shelly and I spent too much of our time arguing over any topic; from not spending enough time together, to finances, to children's issues. We never had to look for things to fight about. There was always something.

"We went through a cycle where the fights got worse and worse until it reached a point where it was unhealthy. We finally reached a crossroads where we came to the breaking point. Shelly had decided that one more time, one more fight, and it would be all over between us."

Shelly agrees with Glen's assessment. She says, "We had just had too many unhealthy fights. I didn't want to go through it again, and I didn't want our kids to witness any more if it."

Then, one night, the inevitable happened.

Shelly remembers, "It was a Saturday, and we had 'one more fight.' It was probably 'the fight of all fights,' and I simply decided 'that's it.'

"Glen left the house at the conclusion of the fight, which was something he didn't usually do. I said to myself, 'This is my ticket out.'"

Glen got in his car and drove to his office in order to get away from the conflict. His head was spinning with what had just happened. He remembers, "As I drove away from our home on the day of the final fight, I remember shaking my head and being so confused. I didn't know what was happening, and I didn't know why it was happening. I was dumbfounded that two people who supposedly loved each other couldn't figure it out.

"But while I was sitting there, God was working on me. I had an anger issue that I couldn't resolve. I don't know why I was angry or why I would treat someone I loved so dearly in the manner in which I did. I didn't understand any of the feelings I was having, and I asked God, 'What's going on? Why can't we just be a normal family? Why can't we just get along?'

"I sat in my office that night, scared and alone, and said, 'God, what's going on? I don't understand what's happening to me... to us.'

"I knew that unless we could turn things around, there wasn't much hope for us as a couple. The fighting worsened and the frequency was intensifying. Something had to change."

Shelly, too, thought that things had to change - and she was convinced that ending the marriage quickly was the right way to change them. She says, "When Glen drove away, my first feeling was one of relief. My primary thought was 'I want out.' My mind was racing. I got the phonebook out and started looking for a hotel for Glen for the night, then an apartment beyond that.

"I immediately started making plans and arrangements. There were so many things going through my mind, but they all centered on how we were going to end this marriage.

"Then, at that very moment, I heard a voice. It said, 'I want you to go apologize.' I immediately thought, 'That can't be God. He wouldn't want me to apologize and continue on like this.'

"Next, God said, 'If you can do this, I will bless your marriage.'

"My immediate response was 'no!' and it came in a very loud voice. I argued with God. I was adamant, 'No way am I doing that!' There was an argument between me and God."

But God won the argument. Shelly got into her car and went looking for Glen. Now she remembers, "As I was driving away from our house, my only thought was, 'I can't believe I have to do this. God, this better be good!'"

"I knew that Glen would be at his office, so I drove there and said, 'I'm sorry.' I said it devoid of emotion. I had no feeling whatsoever because I had hardened my heart long before that. And yet that was the moment when our lives changed."

Glen, too, marks that moment as their turning point. He says, "When she found me in my office and came in, she was stone-faced. I don't remember now if I knew she didn't mean the apology or not. I don't know that it even mattered.

"When Shelly came to me in my office that night, my heart melted. The thing that was so different was that in past fights, when

Shelly would come to me, it was because she still wanted to talk about the issue on her terms."

Shelly agrees. She says, "Part of my agreement with God that night was that I would not only apologize, but that I would say and do whatever it would take to make our marriage work. I would open my heart to what God wanted to teach me. That was the very humbling part for me. However, I think that's what made it all work."

Glen adds, "God had already prepared my heart for Shelly's arrival, but my anger and self-righteousness vanished when she spoke. I didn't hear God audibly, but I am pretty sure He would have said of our fighting, 'This isn't where I want you two to be. This is never what I meant for you.'"

After Shelly apologized, Glen went to her and held her. Then he apologized himself. He said, "Shelly, our lives are going to change from this point forward."

Shelly remembers, "We went home together. Glen sat the boys down at the table and told them he was sorry for the way things had been. Furthermore, he promised them that from that day forward, life would be different. And it was."

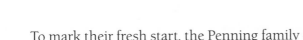

To mark their fresh start, the Penning family decided to try a new church the next morning. Glen and Shelly were both Christians and had been attending church together since high school. Glen explains, "Shelly's family raised her in a Methodist church in Pekin, Illinois. I grew up Catholic, but I was the youngest of eight, so by the time they got to me, my parents were kind of like, 'Hey, whatever works!' I pretty much attended church with Shelly from our early teenage years on. We both grew up in the Methodist church, got married there, and taught Sunday School during our early married years."

The Pennings changed churches when they moved to Moline, Illinois, for work, and then again when they moved to East Peoria. Both times, they became active in their new congregations.

On the Sunday morning after their big fight, the Pennings had no intention of leaving their current church. But its youth program had ended for the summer, so they were interested in finding somewhere to keep their kids active for the summer months. Shelly had heard about what was being done at Willow Creek Community Church outside Chicago and thought it sounded fascinating. When someone told her there was a similar kind of church in Peoria, they had the idea to check out Northwoods during the summer. Before attending that morning, though, they knew very little about it.

Nothing could have prepared Shelly and Glen for what they saw and heard in the Northwoods auditorium that morning. Shelly remembers, "We were confronted with a drama on stage that was a visual re-enactment of the fight we had the night before. It was a hard thing to see.

"The drama showed Satan dressed as a joker and how he could stir things up and add sarcasm into the mix when none was really intended. I could not believe my eyes. Pastor Cal came onto the stage and delivered a message on how God can come into our marriage if we ask Him to.

"Cal concluded the service by asking the husbands in the audience to put their arms around their wives while he taught on how to pray and bring God into our marriages. Glen put his arm around me, and we prayed together that day for the very first time. We have never stopped praying together since, and it has literally changed our lives. Our marriage and our lives changed that day."

Glen says, "It had to be God wanting us to come to Northwoods. We certainly never could have orchestrated that chain of events. The way things fell into place, from God speaking to Shelly to the series being on the topic of marriage to the drama being a re-enactment of our fight... everything was certainly lined up for us.

"All I can say is that I'm glad Shelly listened when He spoke. Considering my stubbornness, I doubt we would ever be where we are today without her obedience. It scares me to think how different our lives could have been."

Shelly agrees. She says, "Without a doubt, Northwoods came into our lives at exactly the right moment. It was the church that put us on the right track. It was the church that taught us how to live a Christian life and what it meant to know Christ and how to walk with Him."

Glen continues, "The timing of the series when we first attended was really unbelievable! It was astounding to sit there as first-timers and see our fight being re-enacted on the stage. I was speechless as the drama progressed. Shelly literally had her mouth open in amazement. Then she started crying. It was quite a memorable welcome to a new church!

"I believe that God speaks to everybody in a different way. Those messages spoke loudly to our hearts. Throughout that series [on marriage], it felt like Cal and I were alone in the auditorium, having a personal conversation. The content of that series was so personal and so targeted for us that Cal couldn't have drafted it any more personally if he had known us for years.

"The problems in our marriage never stemmed from not loving each other. Similarly, it was never a case where our family wasn't important. Our problem was simply that we weren't doing marriage the Biblical way. After listening to Cal, we realized that we were trying to adhere to the culture of the secular world. I was doing everything I could to make more money and be more successful. I was chasing all the wrong things, all the things the world tells you that you need to do.

"We were living a worldly life and merely attending church. We just didn't get it until the day we entered the doors of Northwoods and heard Cal say that Christ needs to be the *head* of every marriage. We understood that Christ needed to be *part* of our marriage, but we didn't have role models or mentors or people actually walking alongside us on the journey.

"Cal's message was pretty blunt that first day. Yet in all our years of attending other churches, I don't think I had ever heard it taught that Christ needed to be the *head* of every marriage. Perhaps in our younger days, Shelly and I had not been as receptive to Biblical teachings because we were so focused on what the world had to say. But clearly we had never heard the message stated as urgently as we did that day.

"We were challenged in that series to put God first in our marriage and first in all our relationships. Cal also stressed the importance of the husband serving as the spiritual leader of the household. That was one of the many things in our marriage that I had not understood or acted upon appropriately prior to coming to Northwoods.

"I had clearly misinterpreted the meaning of the phrase 'spiritual leader of the household.' I never wanted to step on Shelly because I loved her and treasured her strong personality. Shelly has great ideas, but instead of complementing each other, it seemed like we butted heads too often.

"In the end, I had to learn what a spiritual leader was. It is critically important that we, as men, reflect Christ in how we lead. Always keep in mind that Christ was a leader, but never forget that He was a servant leader. Christ laid down His life for us, and in the same way, I have to lay my life down for Shelly. Every family has decisions that must be made, but they need to be made after discussing and communicating both partners' points of view."

————··◦◦◦◦··————

In order to learn more about the concept of the husband as the spiritual leader of the household and to begin what Shelly refers to as "the next phase" of their "marriage rehabilitation," the Pennings began reading Christian books together. Among others, they studied *Love and Respect* by Emerson Eggerichs, *Divorce-Proof Your Marriage* by Gary and Barbara Rosberg, *His Needs, Her Needs* by Willard F. Harley, *Fight Fair* by Tim and Joy Downs, and *How to Speak Your Spouse's Language* by H. Norman Wright.

Shelly says, "It was apparent we didn't know how to do the marriage thing correctly, so we turned to Christian authors and books for guidance. We read books together and sat calmly and actually discussed how we were going to work things out. We were finally learning to communicate and work together."

Through reading, Glen feels that he and Shelly were both able to gain perspective on the factors that had caused them to fight in the first place. He says, "We had been through many of the things that young couples with children experience. We had been through job changes and a move to another city and then back again. There were certainly life factors that contributed stress to our marriage, but clearly the main problem was our refusal to turn over the reins and have God lead our lives.

"My biggest problem personally was a lack of self-control. I manage people daily and now have a great relationship with our kids and with Shelly, but to this day I don't think I have enough self-control to totally control myself and my actions without the grace of God. I must rely on the power of God even today to keep control of myself.

"I still get angry, as do most people. But it's how I handle the anger that makes all the difference. With God's help, I can now sit down and say, 'Shelly, I'm not happy with this or that' or 'I'm feeling really stressed out at work.' Rather than explode, we can talk through things and both come away feeling like we have shared our hearts. It completely changes one's perspective."

The Pennings agree that Christ-centered communication is the key to their improved marriage. Shelly says, "Like any couple, we still have an occasional disagreement. But now we handle it so much differently. Now if there is something we need to discuss, one of us will go to the other and say, 'There is something that's been bothering me, and I would like to talk to you about it.'

"We will hold each other's hand and explain our feelings. I may say, 'This is what happened and I want us to be able to talk about it.' Then we will have a simple conversation without accusations. Unheated, two-way conversation gets everything out in the open. We can discuss our feelings and move on."

Glen, too, is eager to talk about how they have grown. He says, "One of the things I've learned, as far as not projecting my anger onto Shelly, is to always remember that she is God's child. She is special in God's eyes, and who am I to treat her any less than the way God wants her to be treated? If we keep in mind that our spouse is also a person in Christ, then we come at things from a very different perspective.

"Understanding that Shelly is a great believer in Christ helps to show me the perspective that she will approach a problem with. That is a lot different than when I used to think that she was being controlling or manipulative. Now I understand that she is coming from her heart and that she isn't interested in harming me, but only wants to build us.

"In retrospect, our fights were simply odd. We could be arguing about something, and five minutes into the fight, I wouldn't even know what we were fighting about. Like lots of men, I was a great stonewaller. So even if we weren't fighting at least weekly, I was stonewalling my feelings from our last fight and keeping those feelings alive.

Shelly concurs with Glen's assessment. She says, "Our fights were really about how we fought. Each battle would dredge up feelings from previous fights, and they just got worse and worse."

Glen continues, "Finally we had to admit that we weren't doing such a great job of running our own lives. I had to look at myself critically and realize that I didn't have the power the stop the fights myself. It was like something outside of us took control and made this endless cycle happen repeatedly. It took God to say, 'Stop!' I totally believe that Shelly's obedience in listening to God was the trigger to all these events."

For years after their explosive fighting ended, the Pennings simply focused on keeping their own marriage healthy. According to Shelly, "We attended as many workshops as we could on the topic of marriage and even went on the first marriage cruise that Northwoods offered. The cruise was how we celebrated our 20th anniversary."

But gradually, God began to lay a new burden on Shelly and Glen's hearts. After learning how to strengthen their own marriage, the Pennings began to feel called to help other couples with troubled marriages.

Glen says, "It really hurts our hearts to see couples struggling. It saddens us when we go to a restaurant and see couples who are married but living emotionally separate lives and not really communicating. That's not God's design for marriage. The Bible speaks frequently about how marriage should be. Hopefully Shelly and I can be resources which help bring Biblical teachings to people's marriages."

The Pennings began their marriage ministry in their home in 2008. Its numbers then grew so large that they moved it to a local school conference room. They also volunteer as mentors at Northwoods, are presenters at Marriage Encounter workshops, and do individual marriage consulting for couples.

Shelly says, "We don't usually tell the people in the classes we teach about our story. However, we had our biggest group yet in the summer of 2010, and when we were teaching on communication and conflict resolution, I thought it was important to let our group know our story. It helped for them to see that we have been through hard times but have survived and thrived. I believe it helped them open their hearts for some healing in their own marriages."

Glen would never have expected their lives to take this direction, but he's thrilled with what they're doing. He says, "I laugh at where we are today because now we are doing marriage ministry. I have to trust it was God's wish to have iron sharpening iron and to have us go through those hard times to fully prepare us to help others. The interesting thing is that even though we are teaching the fundamentals of marriage, we are still growing in our own marriage.

"With our 25th anniversary coming up, I think we'll actually celebrate it with a trip to become certified marriage consultants. Family Dynamics does a training program in North Carolina, and that's what is ahead on our radar screen. We feel like part of our obedience to Christ has been to put Him first in our marriage. Now it's time for us to take what we have been able to do and share it with others."

Marriage ministry is not the only way God has provided Glen and Shelly the opportunity to share their faith. After teaching them the lesson of obedience to Him in their marriage, He asked them to obey in their professional lives as well.

Glen and Shelly grew up in Pekin, and Glen was active in the park district there. They both loved the family activities that were available in Pekin. After moving to East Peoria, they met with both the city and park district and asked them to put in a miniature golf course as a family activity for all the citizens of East Peoria.

Shortly after that conversation, the Pennings were at church and heard Pastor Cal give a message entitled *Leap of Faith*. Glen remembers, "He taught a sermon that said if you have something on your heart, then it is essential that you trust in God to provide the way for you to accomplish whatever it is."

Shelly chimes in, "When Cal delivered that message, I looked at Glen, and he looked at me, and we both said, 'Oh no. Surely he's not expecting us to do this!' But we did it."

In 2005, the Pennings opened ROC Ice Cream and Golf in East Peoria. Glen says, "We borrowed the name 'ROC' from something that was done at Northwoods called 'Team ROC.' ROC stands for 'Reflections of Christ,' but we use it as a play on words because we have a large boulder and fountains and things like that."

God has used ROC to grow the Pennings' marriage ministry and to bless the families of East Peoria. Shelly says, "ROC is where we really started our marriage mentoring ministry in our home. We would advertise there and say, 'Please come to our home.' We try to spread Christ to everyone who enters ROC. We have Christian music playing and we try to make it a Christ-like atmosphere."

Glen adds, "And Shelly is a magnet for young girls and young women who are struggling with a variety of issues. They'll come in and talk to her about nearly anything. It's the oddest thing when girls come in to get ice cream and end up pouring their hearts out to Shelly about anything and everything. She is just so easy to talk to and so welcoming. She has a Christ-like approachability that is really amazing."

Shelly concludes, "ROC is also a front door for getting couples to connect with us for our home marriage ministry. It really can't even fit in our home anymore. We grew to about 10 couples, and that was the limit in our home. Our last one, which reached 20 couples, had to be held in a rented school room."

In their classes, Glen and Shelly stress the principles of a Biblical marriage. When asked what makes for a strong marriage, Glen says, "To borrow from Ephesians 5 and author Emerson Eggerichs, it's all about love and respect. Before, I simply didn't love Shelly the way she deserved to be loved, and she didn't respect me the way I needed to be respected.

"It's not natural for the man to love. It's completely natural for the woman to love, but it's unnatural for the man. And the same is true in reverse with respect. We didn't understand that important principle when we were fighting.

"Read the Bible and it's all there! God told us how to have good marriages. God told us how to foster good relationships. We just didn't listen!"

Looking back on the day of their last big fight in 1993, the Pennings feel incredibly blessed by how far they have come in the past 18 years.

Glen reflects, "From that day forward, we put God in the driver's seat of our marriage. It's interesting to look back and see all the things we did as a young family trying to be happy. We grew up in a church and had been part of a church throughout our married lives, but we had never put God in charge or been truly obedient to Him.

"Shelly's obedience is what really deserves the credit for saving our marriage. Had she not been obedient that night, the cycle would have reached its end. The fights were like a snowball rolling downhill. Half the time we didn't even know what they were about. We just knew they were unstoppable and growing in intensity in very unhealthy ways.

"A lot of people say you have to pursue God, but I think it's pretty clear that in our situation, God was pursuing us. Shelly readily admits that it was hard for her to obey God that evening and that her words of apology lacked sincerity, but I believe God knew her words were needed to melt my heart."

In her obedience that first night, Shelly kept her marriage together. In their continued obedience, their marriage has grown to be a blessing to countless others.

Glen concludes, "God has truly blessed our family. Through our obedience to the Lord, we have been blessed beyond measure. And now our children are reaping the benefits. We welcomed our first grandchild on November 27, 2010. It's amazing the legacy that we as a family can have, and it's all because we obeyed when God called us to be obedient.

"We totally look forward to what God has in store for us next. Whatever it is, we're signing up for it and saying, 'God, take us wherever it is You want us to go.'"

———··◄❧►··———

It's sobering to realize how different Glen and Shelly's lives would be today, both for themselves and their children, had they not allowed God to bring healing to their hearts and their marriage.

But because they obeyed God and stayed together, one day long after they are gone, the mantel over the fireplace in their adult children's homes will contain a picture of Glen and Shelly, a picture that will be worth more than a thousand words. It's a picture that will continue to whisper: "Love your spouse as Christ loved the Church." It's a picture that will continue to testify, for all time, that God can fix broken marriages.

Financial Clean-Up

Scott's Story

"Audacious faith isn't some newfangled, extra-biblical variety of faith. It's a return to the core of Christianity: trusting Jesus completely in every area of your life and setting out to devote your life wholly to revealing His glory in this world."

SUN STAND STILL BY STEVEN FURTICK

Some time ago, I came across a rather humorous radio program in which one man was being held up by another man in an attempted robbery. With a gun shoved into the victim's ribs, the assailant demanded, "Your money or your life." When his request was met with silence, the robber repeated his request even more forcefully, "Did you hear me? I'm not messing around! Your money or your life!" At which point, the not-so-willing victim said, "Don't rush me; I'm thinking."

The truth is that sometimes our money can have such a tight control on our lives that it clouds our thinking as to what is really important in life. In Matthew 6:19-21, Jesus Christ sought to deliver us from cloudy thinking about money when He said, "Do not store up for yourselves treasure on earth, where moth and rust destroy, and where thieves break in and steal. But store up for yourselves treasures in heaven, where moth and rust do not destroy, and where thieves do not break in and steal. For where your treasure is, there your heart will be also."

Then in verse 24, He laid the matter out in no uncertain terms: "No one can serve two masters. Either he will hate the one and love the other, or he will be devoted to one and despise the other. You cannot serve both God and money."

I have discovered in my own life that money, unlike anything else, can often pose as a rival god. It can summon our allegiance, promise us security and happiness, and cause us to make our decisions in life based solely upon how it will affect our stockpile. Saying "no" to its incessant demands requires a fierce loyalty to the one true God and a commitment to manage one's financial resources with a kingdom mindset.

Scott Cramer was pursuing the American dream, and financing most of it with credit, until God interrupted him in an amazing way. His story is a powerful testimony to the fact that God can break debt's grip on our lives and release us into amazing financial freedom if we will surrender to His wisdom in our money management. But as with Scott, God has something more in mind for us than mere financial freedom. He wants us to be free to pursue His plans and purposes in our lives, and in doing so, to discover spiritual rewards and riches that money can't buy.

Scott Cramer had every reason to be happy with the way his life was going.

He and his wife, Jena, had both been raised in strong Christian homes. He says, "We both accepted Christ as our Savior when we were children. We met at a Christian university and after marriage, we settled into a 'normal' Christian life. I was very involved with a church in our hometown of Galesburg. For about 16 years, we were busy 'doing' church. We were involved in every area. We were adult Sunday School teachers, children's Sunday School teachers, small group leaders, members of the Deacon's Board, members of the evangelism committee, and members of the building committee... you name it, we were in it."

Scott also had a good, steady job. His family owned First Glass in Galesburg, which his father had started when Scott was 8 years old. Scott loved working there with his brother Tim and being part of the family business.

When Scott and Jena began their family in 2000 with the birth of their son Skylar, they began to think seriously about settling into their "forever" home. Jena left her job as a public school teacher to stay at home with the baby, but they went ahead and bought land and began building on Scott's salary.

They built their home in Dahinda, Illinois, south of the lake community in Oak Run. The house was completed in June of 2001, just 10 months before the birth of their second child, a daughter named Clara. The home was absolutely beautiful: a 2,750 square foot house, white with green shutters. It had four bedrooms to fit their growing family. And best of all, it sat on 10 acres of land, perched on a hill overlooking the Spoon River Valley.

Of course, it also came with a hefty mortgage. But Scott and Jena didn't consider this to be a problem. After all, they rationalized, everyone else they knew had a large mortgage too.

In the following years, the Cramers added two more sons to their family: Sterling in 2004, and Evan in 2006.

With four healthy children, a beautiful home, a solid church, and a steady job, it seemed that Scott and Jena Cramer had all they could ask for.

Then, in the summer of 2005, their lives began to change as a result of one small action.

Scott remembers, "Church was a family affair. My parents, my wife and I, our four kids, my brother Tim and his wife, all went to the same service. However, I began to notice that about 15 minutes into the sermon, my brother would get up and walk out. He would do this nearly every week.

"During the week, when we were working together, I'd say to him, 'What are you doing? For the sake of your wife and family, you can't sit there and listen to the message?'

"And he said to me, 'No, I can't. It's a waste of my time.'

"I began to realize that for my brother, time was very, very valuable. As soon as Tim perceived that something was wasting his time, whether it was a relationship, or a conversation, right or wrong, tactful or not, he would move on. At the same time, I noticed that instead of spending his Saturday afternoons and evenings golfing or going out to dinner with friends, he was driving to Peoria and taking his family to church."

"One day when we were on our way to a job site, I asked him about it.

"He said, 'I found this church in Peoria called Northwoods. I'm getting something out of it.'

"I had to see what this was all about. Anyone who thinks like my brother, but is still willing to take a chunk of time out of his Saturday for a church an hour away, must have really found something. We made the visit one Saturday night and were hooked. What Tim had found was passionate worship and relevant teaching. I was moved to tears just about every time we went. We didn't realize we were starving for that. We couldn't get enough. Saturday and Wednesday nights our family made the trek from the Galesburg area to Peoria.

"We did this for a year while still serving at our old church in Galesburg on Sundays. For us, church started on Saturday afternoon at four o'clock and ended Sunday afternoon about one o'clock. It was exhausting.

"As we began to compare the two churches, Jena and I realized that as we raised our young children, we had to be very, very careful that our children didn't perceive us as just 'going through the motions.' We wanted church to be more than just a religious act. If we wanted our kids' relationship with Jesus Christ to be real, then we had to be authentic and passionate about our worship. We couldn't fake it. It had to be real.

"Jena and I realized Northwoods was a place where we could get excited about following Jesus again, and where our kids could see our enthusiasm.

"In the summer of 2006, we knew we needed to make a choice. Either we were going to commit to taking our family to Northwoods and get involved there, or we were going to do our best to serve in our old church and make the best of our situation.

"We prayed hard for three months. We had been at our old church for 16 years. We had lots of close relationships. It would have been easier if we'd been upset with something our church had done. But we weren't. There was nothing wrong with that church. They were ministering to people in the community. New people were getting saved and baptized. But God was putting a holy discontent in our hearts that could not be ignored.

"God made it very clear that He was calling us to worship and serve with a new body of believers at Northwoods. We wrote a letter to the pastors and elders at our former church to explain our decision. We also met with one of the pastors and explained that just as God can call a pastor to a new congregation, He was calling us to a new body of believers.

"It was one of the hardest things we've ever done, but we knew that it was right and we obeyed. God was calling us to something new. We could never have imagined how that first step of obedience would lead us to a string of opportunities to obey God! He has shown His faithfulness and His desire to use us in a new plan.

"I know it didn't make sense to many of our friends in Galesburg. They would say, 'You're going to drive an hour each way to go to a "seeker" church?' Sometimes people use 'seeker church' as a Christian slam to mean 'you're less mature in the faith than we are.'

"We heard comments about Northwoods being 'watered-down religion.' I didn't understand that. Jesus Christ and His crucifixion... how do you water that down? It's either the Gospel or it's not. But we didn't care about the comments. We were being fed at that 'seeker' church more in the first few months than we ever were before at a 'mature' church. We knew that God wanted us to obey and go to Northwoods Community Church.

"Once we got there, God really began to heal our hearts. I felt rescued. Little did I know God was 'rescuing' us so that He could eventually 'wreck' us for His purpose!"

Shortly after the Cramers committed to making Northwoods their church home, Pastor Cal did a series on getting out of debt. Scott vividly remembers that during one message, Cal held up a book by Dave Ramsey entitled *Total Money Makeover*. Seeing that book began another huge phase of change for the Cramer family.

Scott recalls, "We had built a beautiful home on the hill, but we were up to our necks in debt. We had every type of debt: credit card debt, car loans, student loans, a mortgage, and a home equity loan. We had leveraged ourselves to the tune of about $130,000 in the hole.

"We weren't really doing anything differently than anyone else. We weren't bad or behind on any payments. We were just living the American Dream. All of our friends were the same way. Everybody we knew was in debt, many of them deeper in the hole than us. It was 'normal.' But we were tired of 'normal.' God was asking us to be 'different.'

"We read *Total Money Makeover* and did everything Dave Ramsey prescribed: the Emergency Fund, the Debt Snowball, the whole thing. We worked hard. We took extra jobs, we held garage sales, we sold stuff on eBay, and the kids wore consignment clothes. I can still remember bringing home a pair of boots for my oldest son. Skylar was seven at the time. He looked down at the boots and, with disappointment on his face, looked up at me and said, 'It's ok, Daddy... I don't mind used shoes.' Those were humbling times. Beans and rice, rice and beans.'

"One night, after the kids had gone to bed, Jena and I were in the living room. She was reading and I was doing the math on when we would finally be out of debt. I said, 'Hey Jena, you know how you want to remodel the basement?'

"'Yes,' she replied.

"'You know how you want to do the driveway real nice?'

"'Yeah.'

"'You know how you want to do some really nice landscaping out front?'

"'Sure babe, what's up?'

"'I'm sorry, but it's not going to happen. It's mathematically impossible. Add that to putting the kids through college and doing some of the things we want to do as a family...'

"Finally I said, 'Do you realize we're going to be eating beans and rice until we're 75?'

"We had put all our blood, sweat, and tears into this great new home that we had built four or five years before. We sat there and faced the reality that to be free of debt and to be all that God wanted us to be, to completely rely on Him, meant that we had to let go of the house.

"We didn't like doing it, but we sold the house. We took the equity and bought an old re-possessed home in Oneida. It put us another 30 minutes further away from church, but we bought it for $35,000. We completely remodeled it, paying cash for everything."

The Cramers' "new" house was built in 1908. Its 1,800 square feet were "a complete gut job," says Scott. They had to put in new insulation, new drywall, new electrical, new plumbing, and new HVAC. "In the end," says Scott, "it was like a new house on the inside, with 100-year-old bones on the outside, and all paid for." The sale of their house in Dahinda covered all of their expenses.

Scott says, "We paid off everything and haven't been in debt since. Freedom. Finally. That's a great feeling, not owing anything to anyone.

"These days, it's cool to be debt-free. But when we started that journey, everyone thought we were crazy. Our friends surely thought, 'You want to get out of debt? You're nuts! Everyone has debt. You can't get ahead without leveraging debt.'

"'Do you know what you have when you don't have bills?' Dave Ramsey asks on his radio program. 'Money!' And he's right. We didn't have a lot, but for the first time ever, we had a positive net worth."

And all of this was part of God's plan. Because as soon as the Cramers started to save up a little bit of money, God showed them what He wanted them to do with it.

Scott remembers, "We look back on our journey to financial freedom and realize that God was bringing us to a point where He could move us a little bit deeper into another call on our lives that would require faith and obedience. That call was for our family to adopt.

"Starting in December 2007, every book I read, every magazine article I picked up, every radio program I listened to, every message at Northwoods, everything made an impression on me in the aspect of adoption. God was 'nudging' my heart. But we had four kids already! We'd just downsized to a smaller house! What would Jena say?

"One night, lying in bed, just as Jena's head was hitting her pillow, I decided to find out. I said, 'I think God is calling us to adopt.'

"I didn't know what she would say. I expected, 'Go to sleep! You're crazy!'

"Instead, she responded, 'I think so too.'

"So God had been working on both of us independently and in different ways, but we came together in a bedtime conversation and agreed that the next day we were going to take the first step toward adoption.

"I remember going to Lutheran Social Services to start the ball rolling and by filling out some paperwork. The lady sat me down and handed me this brochure. It was several pages long and had pictures of these kids. Next to each picture were a name and a description. I felt like I was leafing through a real estate brochure, except it was for kids. In that moment, God sealed the deal. He wrecked my heart for the fatherless.

"The journey of our adoption story is enough for an entire book. It was an incredible faith-building journey. Again, God called us to obey. We said 'yes' and He provided all that we needed, both financially and emotionally. Spiritually, it was the richest time of my life.

"When we chose our future daughter, Hana, we knew that her mental assessment scores, which were taken in the orphanage in Ethiopia, were at the level of mental retardation. Typically a child will go from the orphanage to a care center, where they will spend three months before the parents come to pick up their child.

"Hana had previously been chosen by another couple, so she had made the trip to the care center, and then the parents backed out. Then she was chosen again. But again, because of the unknown condition that caused her low mental assessment scores, the potential parents backed out. She had been waiting at the care center for a year and a half, watching new kids come in and parents come and pick them up.

"She was on the 'waiting child' list. The list was for kids who had disabilities, seizures, unknown conditions, or troubling behaviors. We prayed about our adoption. We went forward after one service at

Northwoods and asked Cal to pray for our discernment and wisdom. Then we chose Hana and didn't back out.

"In January of 2009, Northwoods started their first 21-day corporate fast. During this time we changed what and how we ate and made hearing God our first priority. Some days we would skip all our meals for the day and just pray during mealtime. Other days we would skip breakfast and lunch and have a 'Daniel Fast' meal of fruits and vegetables.

"During the 21 days of the fast, Jena and I prayed specifically for Hana's development. We saw God answer us incredibly through that period. Hana's mental assessment scores doubled and her behavior improved. Before, she hadn't been able to potty train. Now she was only wearing a Pull-Up at night. She began to communicate with her caregivers and some of the other children.

"There is no question that during those 21 days, when we prayed specifically for Hana, God answered our prayers. I still have copies of Hana's test results from before and after the fast. If you look at them, you would think you were looking at two different kids."

The Cramers brought Hana home from Ethiopia in July of 2009. Although the orphanage does not keep good records of age, they estimate that she is about five months younger than her brother Sterling. Hana fits beautifully into her new family. Three months after the adoption, Scott wrote on their family's blog, "I'm convinced that Hana was meant to be part of our family. There is no doubt…. In fact, it may very well be because Clara is the perfect sister for her."

Certainly, the Cramers had been through four years of huge life change. Scott laughs as he looks back on it. He says, "We'd left our church, sold our dream home, and gotten out of debt. And then, with four biological kids living in a three-bedroom house, God called us to adopt. My parents thought we'd officially lost our minds!"

———— ·‹∞›· ————

But God wasn't done reshaping the Cramers' lives. Even as Scott began to settle into the routine of parenting five children and running First Glass with his brother, the Lord began to tug at Scott's heart once more.

Scott says, "We began to assess the 62-mile-long one-way trek we made every weekend to Northwoods. Church was great. We were getting fed spiritually, and God had clearly changed our lives. He had been moving through the ministry of Northwoods to encourage us to be obedient to the Holy Spirit's leading.

"We always look back to that first step of obedience, leaving our old church, and say, 'What if we hadn't obeyed?' It would have been so much easier just to stay at our church in Galesburg. What if we hadn't obeyed? We wouldn't have gotten out of debt and we wouldn't have adopted Hana. It was amazing and exciting to see God choose to bless those steps of obedience in such a fantastic way.

"But then God started tugging at us again, and we began to think about how we were driving an hour to church and an hour back home. We were driving past all our neighbors and saying, 'Hey, come and join us at Northwoods. It's awesome! God's working there and doing some incredible things.'

"They would kind of look at us and say, 'That's good, but it's too far.'

"We analyzed our situation and said, 'Northwoods is great and it's changed our lives, but what does the "local" church look like? How can we have a local expression of church, even if it means doing Northwoods only on the weekends? What are we doing for our neighbors? What are we doing for our community?' So that was how we started thinking about different ways we could reach out to our community.

"We began to pray about it. One day I was sitting in the Northwoods auditorium and God gave me another 'nudge.' He said, 'What about a simulcast? Northwoods has done simulcasts with Maximum Impact and with the Leadership Summit. What about doing a simulcast every week for your neighbors?'

"So the next morning, I decided I would just put the thought out there. My thinking was, 'If God's put this on my mind and if this is His idea, I'm going to follow through. God's proven His faithfulness in every area leading up to this point. The least I can do is throw an e-mail out there, and then I can be done.'

"My e-mail to Cal was very brief. I'm not sure I even signed it. I had only met him on two occasions, and I was pretty certain he didn't remember me. We had played pick-up basketball once, and Jena and I had gone forward for prayer when we were thinking about adopting Hana.

"The e-mail said, 'Galesburg. Multi-site. Pray about it.' That was the whole thing. I honestly thought that when I hit 'send,' my job was done. I didn't really expect a response.

"But Cal responded in less than 24 hours. I got an e-mail back, saying, 'It's funny you should say that. I've been thinking the same thing. Let's talk.'

"At that time, Jena and I were in a small group with families from four different churches. Our families clicked well and were all kind of investigating what the future might hold for our families with church.

"When I received Cal's e-mail, I was sitting around a table with a group of friends from that small group. I read it and said, 'You're not going to believe this. I just got a response from Cal.' They were all shocked and said, 'No way!'

"The original meeting to discuss a Northwoods multi-site included three couples from Galesburg, Dave Murphy (an elder at

Northwoods), Steve Shaffer (an Executive Pastor), and Cal. Those of us from Galesburg were fascinated with the idea that Northwoods would consider it and even entertain the conversation.

"There was very little commitment that night. It was mostly, 'That's interesting. Now we know where you're coming from.' And then it was over. It left us with a hope that maybe there was a possibility, which needed to be pursued until it became a 'no.'"

Scott didn't hear anything further about the idea for a while, so he thought the concept might have fallen off of Northwoods' radar. But later that fall, Cal called and asked him to round up a few Galesburg Northwoods' attendees for a night of pizza and conversation with some church elders. Scott got together five Galesburg couples who were making the weekly drive to Northwoods, and they all met with Cal and the elders at the Pizza House in Galesburg.

Scott remembers, "At dinner, Cal said, 'Will you guys just go around the room and tell us what Northwoods means to you? What has it done for your faith journey?'

"One by one, everyone talked about how God had just grabbed hold of their lives through Northwoods' ministry. People were getting out of debt, relationships were being healed, unchurched family members were attending, and children were excited about coming to church.

"It was unbelievable. I didn't know any of the stories but my own. All I knew about those people was that they attended Northwoods, just like we did. That night was an emotional time. There were tears and there was laughter. But it was evident that God had used the ministry of Northwoods to change lives.

"When we finished going around the room, Cal thanked us for coming and said we were excused so that they could have an elders' meeting. He told me later that the conversation that night had just lit a fire in everybody and increased their desire to do something in Galesburg."

"Following that night, there were periods of time when I didn't hear anything. I sent Cal an e-mail saying, 'I just want you to know that you don't have to keep me in the loop. In fact, if I'm just the seed dropper, that's great. But if there is anything you need in either Galesburg or Peoria, I'm all in!'

"I wanted Cal and the elders to know that I wasn't a guy who needed to be invited to meetings, but that I was available and happy to do whatever they needed.

"In January 2010, Northwoods did another 21-day fast. During that time, I experienced a clear call that God wanted me to be willing to do more than I had been thinking about previously. In my mind, I figured this meant I needed to promote myself from 'sidewalk shoveler' to 'door greeter.' I remember responding to God, 'OK, Lord, I'm willing.'

"In late January, after the fast, Cal called me at 8 o'clock in the morning on a Wednesday. Monday and Tuesday had been rough days. Sales were down. That day was going to be busy. We really had to crank it out.

"I missed the call. But on the message, Cal asked if I could join him for lunch. I caught up with my brother, who was back in the shop. We had just purchased my dad's shares of the company the month before.

"I yelled into the shop and said, 'Cal needs me to come to Peoria for lunch today. I think it's about the simulcast idea.'

"'There's no way it can happen today,' my brother yelled back.

"'I know,' I said.

"When I called Cal back, I told him how important that particular day was to our end-of-the-month figures. There was no way I could get there. There was silence on the other end of the line. He didn't even respond to my comment. Feeling a little uncomfortable, I broke the silence. 'I could maybe be there at 4:30,' I said.

"Cal said, 'I'll see you then.' Click.

"I hung up the phone and was frustrated. I was thinking that Cal got shot down and wanted me to come over to Peoria to tell me in person that we were done.

"My brother was sitting at the front counter as I walked out the door that afternoon. I'll never forget what he said. He looked at me and said, 'I don't know, but if he offers you a job... take it!' I gave a half-laugh and left.

"The whole way over to Peoria, I was thinking that it had been nice to dream about a satellite in Galesburg, but now that the dream was over, what should my next step be?

"When I got in with Cal, he said, 'We met with the elders last night.'

"'Ok,' I said.

"'And we've voted... to come to Galesburg!'

"My response was, 'Awesome! That's great! Let's get to work! What do we need to do?' I was pumped. Everything we'd been praying for throughout the fast was coming to fruition.

"Cal said, 'We've been talking and we've been praying through the 21-day fast. You were in our top three prayer requests. We wanted to pray for clarity about Galesburg and you in particular. We want you to be "the face of the place."'

"I had no idea what that meant, so I said, 'Okay, that's great.' I was thinking maybe he wanted me to do announcements. In my mind, I was thinking about how God had told me to be ready for more. But I still had no idea what Cal was really saying. I was thinking strictly of a volunteer position, so again I said, 'Great. Let's get to work. What's the next step?'

"Cal said, 'I don't think you understand. I want you to be the face of the place.'

"I was still befuddled, but I said, 'Yep, I gotcha.'

"Finally, he said, 'I'm saying that I want you to leave your company and come on staff full-time.'

"I froze. I was blown away. It took me a while to process because it came absolutely out of nowhere for me. That was nowhere on my radar screen. I wouldn't have thought to put a job application in at Northwoods. I never even considered it to be an option.

"I'm not exactly sure what I said, but I know I told Cal that I needed to talk to my wife and pray about it. He said he thoroughly understood, but he added, 'I know you'll make the right choice.' Cal thought it was a no-brainer, but I wasn't so sure."

———◆———

"Tim and I had just bought my dad out, and everything business-wise had always been me and my brother. My whole thought process was, 'I can't leave my brother and my mom.' I felt like they depended on me. I just couldn't see it being a successful transition if I left them right after Tim and I bought the business.

"On the way home, I called Jena and told her Galesburg was a 'go.' I also told her that Cal had offered me a job as a campus pastor. She didn't believe me, and there wasn't anything I could say on the phone to make her believe me. I couldn't convince her, so we hung up.

"Then I called my brother and said, 'Tim, do you remember when I was walking out the door and you said that if Cal offered me a job, I should take it?'

"He said, 'He offered you a job, didn't he?'

"I said, 'Yes, he did. How did you...?'

"Tim said, 'I didn't. I was frustrated. I had no idea.'

"'I don't think I can take the job,' I said. 'I can't hang my brother out to dry. This is the family business. We're in this together.'

"'Scott, are you crazy?' he asked. 'It is 17 degrees outside, and I just replaced a windshield in a barn. Is this what you want to do for the rest of your life?'

"That was really the moment when I knew. To have my mom and my brother onboard instantly was such a blessing. It wasn't that they didn't recognize the difficulty in the transition. It's that they wanted this so much that if they had to give up their business partner to get Northwoods in Galesburg, then they'd do it.

"That's how all of the Northwoods people I come in contact with in Galesburg are. 'What does it take? What do you need?' Northwoods is going to have a huge impact in Knox County. Hundreds of families will be changed because of the satellite campus we're getting ready to launch. It's going to be the biggest thing in Galesburg. I really believe that.

"When I got home, Jena and I had a longer discussion, and she finally realized it was for real. Then I made a couple of phone calls to some close friends and told them the deal. They said, 'You'd be perfect for it. I can see why he would want you.' That was a very encouraging time, despite my lack of confidence in myself, to hear people I know and respect think I would be right for the job.

"With complete humility, I called Cal, told him I was in, and asked where we would go from there. I didn't ask the salary or anything. He asked how much I made at the time, I told him, and he said, 'Aw, you'll be alright.'

"I had people tell me I needed to negotiate my salary. But my thinking was that God had proven faithful so many times since we made that first step of obedience that I was going to let Him take care of the salary. I wasn't going to negotiate. I'd rather trust that God knows what He is doing and that He will provide.

"That all happened in February of 2010, which gave me four weeks to wrap up everything that I had spent 18 years building at First Glass. On my last day at the shop, it finally hit me. Mom and Tim had gone home, and I started crying. I realized I was leaving a family business that my dad started when I was 8 years old. I was Dad's little helper back then. I began to think of all those years in the business and how this change would be a new chapter in both my life and the life of Northwoods Community Church and its ministry.

"The impact that Northwoods can have, by leveraging technology and raising up new leaders, is exponential. It's exciting to think about how this could be implemented in other communities. I believe that Galesburg is just the tip of the iceberg for what God wants to do through Northwoods. Our involvement with the church has changed my entire life. I'm still holding on... because I don't think the ride is over. What a journey!"

By the way, just to bring you up to speed with Scott's journey as the Campus Pastor of Northwoods Galesburg: on Easter Sunday of 2011, our church plant held its first service. That Sunday, 635 people showed up to pack out an auditorium that could only hold 450 people. Every seat was filled and more than 50 people had to sit in the lobby and watch the service on monitors.

At the end of the service, when Scott got up to call people to a commitment to Jesus Christ, over 65 people made first-time commitments to our Lord and Savior. Needless to say, we were all stunned by what God did on that Sunday and have been amazed to watch His ongoing transformation in the lives of people who are attending this new church in Galesburg.

Today, Scott can only shake his head in wonderment and amazement at what God has done since that day several years ago when he sensed God saying, "Your money or your life." What an incredible journey it's been since the days of "rice and beans." And friend, I want to remind you again that Scott's story can be your story as well if you'll surrender your life, and your wallet, to God and say, "Whatever you want, I'm all in."

When God Doesn't

In this life, we all suffer disappointments. There are times when we don't understand why things in our lives have gone one way instead of another. There are times when we rail against our circumstances and cry out, "It's not fair!" There are times when our hearts ache with despair and we question the Lord, asking, "God, if you CAN do it, then why don't you?"

Disappointment occurs when our expectations clash with the harsh realities of our life experience. Thomas Hutzler relates a humorous story about a father who learned this the hard way. He says, "As ham sandwiches go, it was perfection. A thick slab of ham, a fresh bun, crisp lettuce, and plenty of expensive, light brown, gourmet mustard. The corners of my jaw were aching in anticipation.

"I carried it to the picnic table in our backyard, picked it up with both hands, and was just ready for the first delicious bite, when I was stopped by my wife, who appeared suddenly at my side with our six-week-old son.

"'Hold Johnny,' she said, 'while I get my sandwich.'

"I had him balanced between my left elbow and shoulder and was reaching for my sandwich again, when I noticed a streak of mustard on my fingers. I love mustard... and I had no napkin... so I licked it off. It wasn't mustard.

"No man ever put a baby down faster. It was the first and only time I have ever sprinted with my tongue protruding. With the ends of a washcloth in each hand, I did the sort of routine shoeshine boys do, only I did it on my tongue. Later (after she had stopped crying from laughing so hard), my wife said, 'Now you know why they call that mustard "*Poupon!*"'"

You understand: disappointment in life occurs when your experiences clash with the harsh realities of your actual experience... when you expect mustard and in actuality get something far worse!

While we may laugh at a story like that, the truth is that it's no laughing matter when the clash between expectations and experience is played out in real life and we feel like we got dumped on. It's tough not to question God in those moments when we wonder why He's not doing something to make the situation better.

I'm sure you know exactly what I'm talking about. We've all experienced those painful times in life where we desperately needed God to come through for us and it seemed like He didn't. You prayed, you hoped, you trusted, you believed for the best — and yet, in the end, it's as if God didn't respond. Your prayers went unanswered, your hopes went unmet, or your cries went unheeded. As a result, you may have been left disappointed and disillusioned, wondering why God didn't seem to show up when you needed Him to.

I must admit that I, too, have had my personal wrestling matches with God over why He didn't step in and stop a bad day before it started. There was a day when I held my newborn son in my arms and, in spite of all my prayers for a miracle, I watched in disbelief as the monitors flat-lined and his vital signs closed down. Another time, I watched a brain tumor slowly snuff out my brother-in-law's life, even though I begged God for a miracle to save him. I watched breast cancer slowly end the life of my sister, Carol, in spite of all my pleas for God to heal her.

In times like these, I've identified with Job when he said, in essence, "God, I'd love a personal audience with You right about now, because I'd really like to know what is going on and how it could possibly fit into Your plan."

In his book entitled *Cries of the Heart*, Ravi Zacharias writes, "To live is to sooner or later experience or witness pain and suffering. To reason is to inevitably ponder 'Why?'" In fact, he writes, "I do not know of any question that is asked more, nor of any obstacle to belief that is more persistent."

The Bible doesn't directly answer all of the "why" questions. Instead, it gives us a record of men and women who, like you and me, trusted God, even in the midst of their bad days, and stood firm in their faith in spite of all their questions.

The prophet Habakkuk asked God, "Why do You make me look at injustice? Why do You tolerate wrong?" (Habakkuk 1:3). In Psalm 10:1, David cried out, "Why, Lord, do You stand so far off? Why do You hide Yourself in times of trouble?"

On one of his many bad days, Jeremiah wondered aloud, "Why is my pain unending and my wound grievous and incurable?" (Jeremiah 15:18). And in the midst of overwhelming suffering, Job cried out, "Why have You made me Your target?" (Job 7:20).

Throughout history, people of great faith have asked "why?" That's the question that haunts the secret places of our hearts when our life experiences clash with our expectations of God. We cry out, "God, why, when You could have done something, didn't You?" That's the question that forces its way to the front of our mind on our bad days.

When Dawn Henderson's husband abandoned her, she asked "why?" When Ali Heth died at a young age, her parents cried out to the Lord, asking "why?" As Vicky Johnson's broken foot failed to heal, she wondered "why?" As Shelly and Glen Penning watched their marriage deteriorate, they both ached to know "why?"

Even Jesus, on His bad day, asked the "why" question. As He took upon Himself the sins of the world, for just a brief moment the Heavenly Father had to look away and Jesus felt a sense of utter abandonment. In His humanity, Jesus felt what it was like to be confused by pain and disappointment, and cried out, "My God, my God, why have You forsaken me?" (Matthew 27:46).

Through His desperate cry, Jesus taught us the vast importance of bringing God into our disappointments. God can handle our raw emotions and our questions. He can handle our rants, our tears, and our cries. The important thing is to bring Him into our disappointments and to aim our hard questions at Him rather than excluding Him from our bad days. As I wrote earlier, author Philip Yancey has said, "The alternative to disappointment with God seems to be disappointment without God."

If we walk away from God when life gets tough, we won't be any better off. In fact, we need Him more than ever on the bad days. So how, then, can we manage to stay faithful in the fog of disappointment? First, we need to **Get Clear** about a few things:

First, we need to get clear about the fact that walking by faith doesn't preclude unanswered questions. Following God does not mean that we will automatically understand everything that happens in this world. In fact, precisely the opposite is true. Faith means choosing to trust God in spite of what we don't understand and in spite of our unanswered questions. To be faithful, we must choose to believe that what doesn't make any sense to us still makes perfect sense to God.

Shelly Penning wasn't the least bit happy with God when He told her to go find her husband and apologize to him following yet another of their disagreements. Even though she did not understand why, Shelly drove to Glen's office and obeyed God's command. The result has been a marriage blessed beyond her wildest hopes.

When Scott and Jena Cramer sensed God calling them to a new church, which would require them leaving their established church home, it didn't make any sense to them at first. And then when God called them to move to a smaller house and add a fifth child to the family, they surely thought that God's plan seemed a bit counterintuitive. Yet because of their obedience to His will, their family has been blessed.

We simply cannot make our faith dependent upon our own ability to understand everything. God reserves the right to know many things that we don't know. This means that there are some things we simply will not understand until we get to Heaven. We need to accept that fact by faith so that we won't lose heart when our bad days leave us with unanswered questions.

Secondly, we need to get clear about the fact that walking by faith doesn't exempt us from difficult times. In fact, Jesus warns us that the difficult times will always be present, in spite of our faith. Jesus told His disciples, "In this world you will have trouble. But take heart! I have overcome the world" (John 16:33).

In issuing this warning to His disciples, Jesus didn't intend for them to take on a "woe is me" attitude and become trouble-focused. No, He tells us that we can overcome; we're more than conquerors through His power that is at work within us! But in hard times, it helps to remember Jesus did not promise His followers an exemption from the world's troubles.

Recognizing this, I find it helpful to examine and clarify my expectations from time to time. Do I expect that my faith should keep me from ever having a bad day? Do I expect that just because I'm a Christ-follower, I should never know disappointment or loss? Do I expect that I get an exemption from all the setbacks and disappointments in life?

For now, we are living in what the Bible calls "this present evil age" (Galatians 1:4). While the effects of that evil will touch our lives at times, the truth we need to focus on is that God is always at work for our good. Romans 8:28 says, "And we know that in all things God works for the good of those who love Him and have been called according to His purpose." No matter what we're going through, God is always at work for good, even if His plan is not immediately apparent to us.

Thirdly, we need to get clear about the fact that walking by faith doesn't make us immune to unexplainable tension. Why is it that God seems to miraculously answer prayers at some times, and yet at others He doesn't? Why does it appear that He heals some people, but not others? Why did He save Doug Siefken from his attempt at suicide, yet allow Ali Heth to die in a car accident? Why did He save Mark and Amy Vonachen's marriage, yet allow Dawn Henderson's to fail?

I don't claim to know the mind of God in these specific situations, but my best answer to these questions is that we live in a tension between the "already" and the "not yet." Already the powers of the coming age have broken into this present age, so we expect to see His power on display in amazing ways. And yet, the coming age will not be fully realized in this present evil age until Jesus comes again, so sometimes we will experience setbacks and disappointments.

One of the classic Biblical passages that speaks to this tension is from the "great faith" chapter in Hebrews 11. After running down a list of all the great feats of faith that men and women of the past have accomplished, the author says, "And what more shall I say? I do not have the time to tell about Gideon, Barak, Samson, Jephthah, David, Samuel and the prophets, who through faith conquered kingdoms, administered justice, and gained what was promised; who shut the mouths of lions, quenched the fury of the flames, and escaped the edge of the sword; whose weakness was turned to strength; and who became powerful in battle and routed foreign armies. Women received back their dead, raised to life again." (Hebrews 11:32-35).

As I read that passage, I think about what a mighty God we serve. Nothing is impossible for Him! He wins our battles, quenches the flames, makes us more than conquerors, and even raises the dead. Who wouldn't want to follow a God like that?

I love it when God shows us His power. And often, we expect Him to intervene because His power has broken into this present age. But, we need to understand from the passage we just read that there's more to the story.

The writer of Hebrews continues and shows the other side of faith. He writes, "Others were tortured... some faced jeers and flogging, while still others were chained and put in prison. They were stoned; they were sawed in two; they were put to death by the sword. They went about in sheepskins and goatskins, destitute, persecuted, and mistreated... They wandered in deserts and mountains, and in caves and holes in the ground." (Hebrews 11:35-38).

Yet after this bleak picture, the writer concludes, "These were all commended for their faith!" (Hebrews 11:39). Do you see? The same faith that brought about a great deliverance for some also enabled others to stay faithful to God in the midst of intense suffering and persecution.

Like so many of us, you might ask, "Why does God deliver some and not others?" After years of painstaking research and profound theological analysis, here's my humble answer: "I don't know!"

Sometimes the Lord brings glory to Himself by saying to the world, "Watch this powerful work that I'm going to do **for** this person as I enable him to triumph by faith." At other times, He says, "Watch this powerful work that I'm going to do **in** this person as I enable him to endure by faith."

It's all a part of the faith tension. Sometimes we'll triumph over, and sometimes we'll endure through... but it's always by faith!

In the case of Julie Walker, God did a great work **for** her as He enabled her to overcome her insecurities and gave her a new career. Likewise, He did a great work **for** Vicky Johnson when He healed her broken foot. But God did his work **in** Alan and Lisa Heth as He comforted them in their time of loss. The Lord's work was **in** Rick Jeremiah when his heart became new and he left behind the ways of his old life.

Ultimately, each of us needs to get clear about why we're following Jesus. Is it because He is Lord? Is it because He laid down His life for you, died on a cross for you, gave His all for you, and loves you with a crazy love?

Or is there another reason? Are you following Him because you want Him to make your life better or happier or easier? If this is the reason why, your faith will easily be shaken whenever a bad day comes your way.

I think of a young man who came to faith in Christ at our church a few years ago while he was experiencing the break-up of his marriage. He was in excruciating pain, and I know he came to Christ in the hope that Jesus would fix his marriage. Over and over again, whenever times got tough, he would e-mail me and say, "Cal, it's not working. I don't know if I can continue to follow Him. My faith is failing."

I would always write back and encourage him to hold on to Jesus no matter what. But when his marriage ended, he walked away from his faith in Christ, because he had begun following for the wrong reasons.

We have seen that God can and does fix broken marriages, like in the cases of the Vonachens and the Pennings. But there are also cases in which in spite of our best efforts, marriages fail, as was the case with Dawn Henderson. You see, just because God **can** doesn't mean that He always **will**. Either way, we cannot allow any specific situation to be the litmus test of our faith.

We need to ask ourselves, "Did I come to Jesus because I hoped He would fix something for me? If so, will I walk away if He doesn't?" If you came to Christ for any reason other than the fact that He is **LORD**, your reason won't be enough to hold you when you go through your bad day.

Even if you experience a loss that you can't understand, even if you seek Him for a healing that never comes, and even when your way is dark, you can always trust in God's sovereign plan and amazing love for you. Our faith in Christ is not to be dependent upon whether or not He does everything that we want Him to do. We need to trust Him, walk with Him, and stay faithful to Him, even when we do not understand, simply because He is Lord.

Once we have gotten clear about what it means to follow Him, another step can help us when we are walking through the fog of disappointment. If our first task is to Get Clear, then our second is to **Not Fear**! Over and over again in His Word, God says to us, "Fear Not." And in our dark times, we can rest in Him, not because we know exactly how our bad days are going to turn out, but because we know the reality that God is with us.

God's promise to each of His followers is stated in Hebrews 13:5: "Never will I leave you; never will I forsake you." In the very next verse, we see the application of that truth: "So we say with confidence, 'The Lord is my helper; I will not be afraid'" (Hebrews 13:6).

But not only is God *with* us, He is also *for* us. Romans 8:31 says, "What, then, shall we say in response to this? If God is for us, who can be against us?" In this verse, the word "if" is not meant to convey any doubt. We can read that passage as, "Since God is for you, who can be against you?" The passage continues, "Since He did not spare even His own Son but gave Him up for us all, won't He also give us everything else?" (Romans 8:32). We can lean on the truth of these words and remind ourselves in every bad day that "God is for us!"

When we understand the realities that God is both *with* us and *for* us, we know that no matter what our situation might look like right now, God has a plan to resolve it.

I love the story about the little boy who was reading a cowboy book one evening and started to get anxious because his hero was in dire trouble. That poor storybook cowboy was having a really bad day, and the little guy was sure the cowboy couldn't make it out of his situation alive.

Our little friend got so worried that he finally flipped to the last chapter to see how the story would turn out. To his relief, sure enough, his hero was still alive at the end of the book. That knowledge gave him a sense of renewed confidence as he turned back to that moment of tense activity in the middle of the book.

If you could have listened at the door of his room that night, you would have heard him tell that cowboy, "Hey buddy, I know it's tough right now, but don't give up! I've read the back of the book, and trust me, everything's going to be alright."

And friend, those are exactly the same words that Jesus Christ whispers to each of us today. No matter what you're going through or how bad it looks, He says to you, "Do not fear! I am with you and I am for you." To that, I can add, "I've read the back of the book, and we win! So hang in there — there's a great ending in store!"

Our first step is to Get Clear; our second is to Not Fear; and finally it remains for us **Draw Near**! When we have bad days, we should draw ever nearer to God. James 4:8 says, "Draw near to God and He will draw near to you." I have discovered in my darkest moments that my strength, my joy, and my confidence come from knowing the nearness of His presence. It's not the absence of problems, but rather the nearness of His presence, that enables me to triumph on my bad days.

When we draw near to the Lord, we can rest in the promise that He will carry us through even the darkest days. Psalm 55:22 says, "Cast your cares on the Lord and He will sustain you." Through this verse, we can know that God will give us the support we need to stay faithful to Him as we walk through our bad days.

In his story, Doug Siefken told us that whenever he feels ashamed of his attempt at suicide or feels the old urge to start drinking again, it is God's support that allows him to overcome those negative emotions. In the same way, it was the support from God and His body of believers that helped Alan and Lisa Heth make it through the difficult days following their daughter's death.

When we draw near to God, we receive not only His support, but also His strength. Isaiah 41:10 states, "So do not fear, for I am with you. Do not be dismayed, for I am your God. I will strengthen you and help you; I will uphold you with my righteous right hand." When we draw near to the Lord, we will find renewed strength to withstand our struggles.

But then, we also find that He surprises us at times in the most amazing ways. In answer to Julie Walker's prayers to end her anxiety about performing, the Lord gave her strength and support, but furthermore, He surprised her with more than she had hoped for. Julie wanted the confidence to sing in front of groups; God gave her not only that, but also a career as a songwriter and performer.

God also had surprises in store for Rick Jeremiah, transforming the heavy-drinking former railroad worker into a sound technician who "can't get enough" of church. And then there are Scott and Jena Cramer, who the Lord surprised over and over again: with a new church home when they were already established at one closer to their house, a new daughter from Ethiopia when they thought their family was already complete with four children, and a new career in ministry when Scott had expected to spend his whole life in the family business.

Through these stories, we've seen that God has a way of surprising us when we least expect it. As humans, we sometimes get frustrated or angry with God because we can't see how our bad days will fit into His big picture. But the Bible tells us: "No eye has seen, no ear has heard, no mind has conceived what God has prepared for those who love Him" (1 Corinthians 2:9). There is coming a day when all our disappointments will dissolve in a puddle of tears of joy and wonderment when we see the awesome ending God had in mind for us all along.

So when disappointment has brought some fog into your life, remember that the God who can, **will** bring you through every bad day, and the ultimate ending is going to be worth it all. The only question you need to ask yourself is this: "Have I placed my complete trust in Him, regardless of my circumstances?"

I will never forget the night, 22 years ago, when I sat wrestling with God over the loss of my newborn son. I had plenty of questions for Him, and in answer, He spoke to my heart from a passage in the Bible.

At the end of John 6, many people who were following Jesus for the wrong reasons made the decision to walk away from Him. They had first gone to Jesus because they had personal and political aspirations, and they thought that He could make their lives better in those ways. When they found out that He was actually calling them to lay down their lives, their dreams, and their aspirations to follow Him, they started to think that they'd be better off on their own. John 6:66 says, "From this time, many of His disciples turned back and no longer followed Him."

For those who have come to the Lord under false pretenses, it's only too easy to walk away. You may have come to Him because you wanted Him to restore your marriage, or you hoped He would heal you, or you desired Him to solve some problem for you. And if things didn't turn out like you'd hoped, maybe you said, "Well, I tried Jesus and it didn't help anything. He didn't solve my problem, so I'm done with Him."

See, some people try Jesus because they think He is a magic wand they can wave over their temporal problems. But that's not true faith, and it will only lead to disillusionment.

But if you are looking for someone to walk with you through the trials of life, sometimes delivering you from them and at other times sustaining you through them, then God can! If you are looking for someone to give you hope and a purpose while this earthly kingdom stands, then God can! If you want someone who, when all the kingdoms of this world have one day crumbled, can give you a Kingdom that cannot be shaken, then God can! You see, it's all a matter of what you are looking for.

When others walked away, Jesus looked at His chosen 12 disciples and said, in essence, "Do you guys want to leave too?" (John 6:67). Simon Peter answered Him with the words that each of us must ultimately claim as our own: "Lord, to whom shall we go? You have the words of eternal life. We believe and know that you are the Holy One of God" (John 6:68-69).

So on the night of my son's death, with tears rolling down my face, I prayed, "Lord, I am so disappointed right now. I will never understand why You didn't heal my son. But I know that I don't want to do life without You, nor do I want to confine my hopes solely to this world. So I choose to follow You, no matter what, because I know that You alone can give eternal life."

If you're already His follower, rejoice in making that your claim. And if you've not yet decided to follow Him, I urge you to open yourself up to all the support, strength, and surprises that faith in God can bring.

Afterword

As I was reflecting on the title of this book one day, I found myself remembering a familiar refrain from one of the cheers during my high school basketball days. The cheerleaders would often resort to a particular chorus in order to remind us that no situation was insurmountable if we kept on battling. The rousing cheer went something like this: "Joe, Joe, he's our man, if he can't do it, Tim can! Tim, Tim, he's our man, if he can't do it, Cal can!" And thus it went, through the names of the starting five until they'd come to the final guy. "Curt, Curt, he's our man, if he can't do it, nobody can!"

Basketball cheers aside, the truth is that many times we live our lives as if the realm of possibility is defined solely by what our human efforts can produce. But I have seen God do the seemingly impossible often enough that I would amend that cheer today to say that when you've exhausted the help of man, when the last man standing can't do it... God can!

I hope you have enjoyed this book of real life stories. I would like to take you back, for just a moment, to Shauna Niequist and her book *Bittersweet*. As you may recall from the Foreword, Shauna was encouraging us to "tell our own stories."

She continues, "This is what I want you to do: tell your story. Don't allow the story of God, the sacred, transforming story of what God does in a human heart to become flat and lifeless. If we choose silence, if we allow the gospel to be told only on Sundays, only in sanctuaries, only by approved and educated professionals, that life-changing story will lose its ability to change lives."

Shauna also writes, "If you are a person of faith, it is your responsibility to tell God's story, in every way you can, every form, every medium, every moment. Tell the stories of love and redemption and forgiveness every time you experience them. Tell the stories of reconciliation and surprise and new life everywhere you find them."

Friend, I hope as you've read these stories, they have opened your heart to believe God for what He can and will do in your life. But if you do not yet know God in a personal way, I want you to know that all of His possibilities begin in your life when you place your faith and trust in His Son, Jesus Christ.

God loves you and allowed His Son, Jesus Christ, to die a brutal death on a cross to pay the penalty for your sin, so that you could be forgiven and come back into a relationship with your Heavenly Father. Then God raised Jesus from the dead to give you life, both abundant life right now and eternal life when your time on planet Earth is over.

This Jesus now wants to come and live inside you through the Holy Spirit. But because the Holy Spirit is a Gentleman, He will not force Himself on you. He simply awaits your invitation. If you will invite Him into your heart, Jesus Christ will enter your life, forgive you, change you, and lead you on an exciting adventure with Him. He will do things in you, for you, and through you that may astound you.

Ephesians 3:20 says, "[He] is able to do immeasurably more than all we ask or imagine, according to His power that is at work within us." Friend, that simply means that if His power is at work within you, you aren't even able to imagine what God can do!

So why not invite Him to unleash His power and presence in your life? Just pray this simple prayer in the sincerity of your heart, and you will start a new life with Jesus Christ the moment you do!

"Heavenly Father, thank you for Your incredible love for me that sent Your Son, Jesus Christ, to the cross for me so that I could be forgiven and have an amazing life with You. I now invite You, Jesus Christ, to come into my life, to forgive my sin, and to change me, lead me, and direct me from this day forward. Fill me with Your Holy Spirit and teach me how to love, follow, and obey You. Thank you now for coming into my life and making me a brand new person. I look forward to how You're going to write Your story in and through my life. Please make my life a testimony of what God can do, as I trust and follow You. In Jesus's name. Amen

Friend, we'd love to hear from you. If God has used this book in any way to impact your life, please write and tell us about it at: cal.rychener@nwoods.org.

Discussion Questions

Re-Awakening

1. For Pastor Cal, the Bill Hybels' radio interview was a "defining moment" in his life. Can you think of a time in your life that might be described as a "defining moment"?

2. Have you ever heard, watched or read something that resonated in your heart as a longing or nudge from God? If so, what was it?

3. Faced with a momentous decision, such as Pastor Cal faced in leaving his established church for an uncertain church plant adventure, would you have had the faith to step out into the unknown? Why or why not?

Healing the Wounds of Abandonment

1. Do you agree with Pastor Cal that many of us do not grasp our true identity? If so, why?

2. Dawn felt that God was stirring something within her. Have you experienced a similar feeling? When?

3. When Dawn's marriage started to unravel, her thought was "If God is good, then this wouldn't be happening to me." Have you ever felt that way?

4. Dawn realized, when life seemed most bleak, that God loved her. Why are we often forced to face time in the desert before we see the depth of God's love?

5. How do you explain Dawn's New England beach experience? Has anything similar ever happened to you?

Finding God the Hard Way

1. Doug states, "For 20 years I toiled in a profession I absolutely abhorred." Do you think his drinking and divorce stemmed from his job dissatisfaction or vice versa? Have you found that sometimes life dissatisfaction stems from one root cause?

2. Doug says he can now see that God had a plan for him but waited for his downward spiral to be complete before revealing it. Why do you think so many of us have to hit rock bottom before we turn to God?

3. Doug notes the number of people God put in his path that eventually led to his spiritual awakening. Have you ever had a similar experience - something God-related that happened too often to be a mere coincidence?

4. Doug mentions the ease with which he slid back into drinking. Have you noticed times in your life when sin was hard to avoid?

5. Pastor Cal said, "I want to know what the real Doug Siefken looks like." Do you think all of us have a façade that needs to be shattered?

Making Music Again

1. When a stranger asked Julie's father, "Which one's the star?" the comment pierced her heart and allowed self-doubt and feelings of inferiority to enter. Can you recall similar comments in your life that triggered self-doubt?

2. As Julie got older, she would routinely succeed in anything she tried out for. And yet she continued to have low self-esteem. Do you see anything like this in your life or the lives of those you know?

3. Julie's greatest gift became her greatest struggle. Have you seen this struggle in other people? Explain.

4. Have you ever felt like Julie did when she feared that she would never live the dream and the passion that God had given her? Explain.

5. On selling her successful business and moving on to performing and song writing, Julie says, "In my heart, I felt I was doing the right thing, but the unknown can be scary." Have you ever had similar feelings?

A Part of the Mix

1. Pastor Cal writes about "radical spiritual transformation". Have you witnessed this in yourself or someone else? Explain.

2. Rick's story begins in a hospital room. Where does your begin?

3. The hospital scene happened 36 years ago. Rick says it made "a long and lasting impression." Can you think of a spiritual event that occurred a long time ago and left a lasting impression on you?

4. Rick describes the slow process that ultimately led to his conversion experience. Are any parts of his story similar to yours?

5. Rick says, "I didn't know that God was missing in my life because I was running my own life. I didn't think I needed a higher power telling me what to do." Do you think this is a common sentiment of non-believers?

Living Through Loss

1. Alan stated, "I'm a good guy. I don't drink, smoke, or cheat on my wife. I love my kids and spend time with my family." That was his explanation for why God should favor him. Have you known others who took this approach to their spiritual life?

2. Lisa felt that she was a Christian because "I went to church, had a Christmas tree and believed in Jesus". Have you known others who took this approach to their spiritual life?

3. Alan's first reaction after receiving the news of Ali and Mary's deaths was to pray for strength. What would be your immediate reaction to such tragic news?

4. One of the people who most touched the Heth family was a Virginia Beach neighbor named Chris. He had "tattoos everywhere, a buzz

haircut, body piercings, a big diamond in one ear, the tilted cap and big baggy clothes." Despite his unconventional appearance, the young man had "a huge heart" and was "another one of those miracles that happened along the way." Have you ever regretted judging someone solely on the basis of his or her appearance? Describe.

5. Lisa says, "After Ali died, I knew I had a choice to make. I could be angry and turn from God, or I could be angry and run to Him." Can you relate to her feelings? Comment.

Back on Her Feet

1. Pastor Cal describes a physical healing he experienced at the age of 15. Have you ever prayed for, and received, a physical healing?

2. While she and Cal prayed over Vicky, Leesa insisted "there was something deeper going on" in Vicky's heart. Do you think failing to bring all of our hurts before the Lord can impede His healing work?

3. At the conclusion of the healing prayer time, Vicky says "it literally was like I could feel the hand of Jesus on me." Have you ever had a similar experience?

4. After the healing had occurred, Vicky was still a little cautious and apprehensive. Have you had a similar feeling when God's blessing almost seemed too good to be real?

5. Vicky says, "God is so big that I don't think our small minds can comprehend the vastness of His power." Do you agree with her statement? Why or why not?

Up Out of the Trenches

1. Pastor Cal writes, "For some, it seems that life's trials serve only to harden their hearts and drive them away from God." Have you witnessed this in your life or the lives of others? Explain.

2. After watching them live through three miscarriages, a tragic fire, the death of three members of Amy's family, a new baby, a move,

new jobs, and Mark's deployment to Iraq, we can see the growing turmoil in their home. Have you ever had a similar season of chaos and change?

3. Mark says, "I saw a lot of things I won't forget. I have hauled body bags and done casualty evacuations. Things like that leave a lasting impression." Can you think of a time in your life when things seemed frightening and uncertain?

4. When Mark moved out and thought of ending their marriage, Amy turned to prayer. Have you known a time in your life where the darkness and difficulties drove you to prayer? Explain.

5. Mark exclaims, "When I come into the auditorium, it's like I'm entering a bomb shelter. Everything that has been bombarding me all week long is put on hold." Do you have a "safe place" with God that does something similar for you?

Together... For Better Or Worse

1. Pastor Cal asks, "What kind of picture are our children getting from the marriages they are observing in our homes?"

2. Why would God ask Shelly to apologize? Have you ever apologized, even when you felt you were in the right? What was the result of your apologizing?

3. Glen says, "Our problem was simply that we weren't doing marriage the Biblical way." How many marriages do you think could be saved if couples did them the Biblical way?

4. Glen and Shelly felt they had misinterpreted the concept of the husband being the "spiritual leader of the household." What does this concept mean to you?

5. Shelly says, "We will have a simple conversation without accusations. Unheated, two-way conversation gets everything out in the open." How might this technique help you in your own relationships?

Financial Clean-Up

1. Pastor Cal writes, "I have discovered in my own life that money, unlike anything else, can often pose as a rival god." Do you agree? Explain.

2. Scott says, "If we wanted our kids' relationship with Jesus Christ to be real, then we had to be authentic and passionate about our worship." Do you agree or disagree with this assessment? Explain.

3. Scott and Jena went from having debt of every kind to being debt free. If you currently have debt, what would it feel like for you to be debt free?

4. During the church's 21 day corporate fast, Scott and Jena prayed specifically for the little Ethiopian girl they planned to adopt. Have you had similar experiences with fasting and prayer?

5. Scott feels that his obedience to God's call is what has released God's blessings of financial freedom, a new daughter, and a new career. At the time, each step was a leap of faith. Have you ever found yourself facing a giant leap of faith? How did you react?

Notes

"Foreword"

page 4 – Niequist, Shauna. *Bittersweet: Thoughts on Change, Grace, and Learning the Hard Way*. Grand Rapids, MI: Zondervan, 2010. 237-238. Print.

page 5 – Niequist, Shauna. *Bittersweet: Thoughts on Change, Grace, and Learning the Hard Way*. Grand Rapids, MI: Zondervan, 2010. 239. Print.

"Re-Awakening"

page 8 – Bill Hybels radio interview, March 1988.

"Healing the Wounds of Abandonment"

page 13 – Hosea 2:14, New International Version, 2011.

pages 13-14 - Hamp, Bob. *Think Differently, Live Differently: Keys to a Life of Freedom*. Thinking Differently Press, 2010. Print.

pages 28-29 - Hamp, Bob. *Think Differently, Live Differently: Keys to a Life of Freedom*. Thinking Differently Press, 2010. Print.

"Finding God the Hard Way"

page 31 – Manning, Brennan. *Abba's Child: The Cry of the Heart for Intimate Belonging*. Colorado Springs: NavPress, 2002. 154-155. Print.

page 32 – John 8:36, New International Version, 2011.

page 42 - Matthew 28:19-20, paraphrase.

page 43 – Luke 4:18-19, New International Version, 2011.

"Making Music Again"

page 45 – Littauer, Florence. *Silver Boxes: The Gift of Encouragement*. Dallas: Word Publishing, 1989. Print.

page 45 – Eldredge, John. *Waking the Dead: The Glory of a Heart Fully Alive*. Nashville: Thomas Nelson Publishing, 2003. Print.

page 56 – Julie K. *A Sunny Day*. Splash Records, 2009. CD.

page 56 – Julie K. *Animal Party.* Splash Records, 2010. CD.

page 58 – Matthew 19:26b, New International Version, 2011.

pages 58-59 – Littauer, Florence. *Silver Boxes: The Gift of Encouragement*. Dallas: Word Publishing, 1989. Print.

"A Part of the Mix"

page 73-74 – 2 Corinthians 5:17, New American Standard Bible.

"Living Through Loss"

page 75 – Wilson, Pete. *Plan B: What Do You Do When God Doesn't Show Up the Way You Thought He Would?* Nashville: Thomas Nelson Publishing, 2010. 219. Print.

page 76 – Romans 8:28, New International Version, 2011.

page 76 – John 16:33, New International Version, 2011.

page 76 – Psalm 91:15, New International Version, 2011.

page 98 – Inspiration Quartet. "God Is Still Good." *What A Day.* 2004. CD.

"Back On Her Feet"

page 99 – Batterson, Mark. *In a Pit with a Lion on a Snowy Day: How to Survive and Thrive When Opportunity Roars.* Colorado Springs: Multnomah Books, 2006. 76. Print.

page 104 – Ephesians 6, paraphrase.

"Up Out of the Trenches"

page 109 – James 1:2-3, New Living Translation.

page 109 – Yancey, Philip. *Disappointment with God*. Grand Rapids, MI: Zondervan, 1997. Print.

page 115 – Eldredge, John. *Wild at Heart: Discovering the Secret of a Man's Soul*. Nashville: Thomas Nelson Publishing, 2001. 13. Print.

page 120 – James 1:2-3, paraphrase.

page 122-123 – 1 Peter 5:10, New International Version, 2011.

"Together... For Better Or Worse"

page 125 – Stanley, Charles F. *Living the Extraordinary Life: Nine Principles to Discover It*. Nashville: Thomas Nelson Publishing, 2008. Print.

page 125 – Ephesians 5:22-23, paraphrase.

page 126 – Robert McQuilken's resignation letter from Columbia Bible College, email.

page 134 – Eggerichs, Dr. Emerson. *Love and Respect: The Love She Most Desires; The Respect He Desperately Needs*. Nashville: Thomas Nelson Publishing, 2004. Print.

page 134 – Rosberg, Dr. Gary and Barbara. *Divorce-Proof Your Marriage: 6 Secrets to a Forever Marriage*. Wheaton, IL: Tyndale House Publishers, Inc., 2003. Print.

page 134 – Harley, Willard F. *His Needs, Her Needs: Building an Affair-Proof Marriage*. Old Tappan, NJ: F.H. Revell Co., 1986. Print.

page 134 – Downs, Tim and Joy. *Fight Fair: Winning at Conflict without Losing at Love*. Chicago: Moody Publishers, 2010. Print.

page 134 – Wright, H. Norman. *How to Speak Your Spouse's Language: Ten Easy Steps to Great Communication from One of America's Foremost Counselors*. New York: Center Street, 2006. Print.

page 139 – Ephesians 5, paraphrase.

page 139 – Eggerichs, Dr. Emerson. *Love and Respect: The Love She Most Desires; The Respect He Desperately Needs*. Nashville: Thomas Nelson Publishing, 2004. Print.

"Financial Clean-Up"

page 141 – Furtick, Steven. *Sun Stand Still: What Happens When You Dare to Ask God for the Impossible*. Colorado Springs: Multnomah Books, 2010. 40. Print.

page 141 –*The Jack Benny Program*. Writ. John Tackaberry and Milt Josefsberg. NBC. 28 March 1948. Radio.

page 142 – Matthew 6:19-21, New International Version, 1984.

page 142 – Matthew 6:24, New International Version, 1984.

page 147 – Ramsey, Dave. *The Total Money Makeover: A Proven Plan for Financial Fitness*. Nashville: Thomas Nelson Publishing, 2003. Print.

page 151 – Cramer, Scott. "Oh yeah… we have a blog to update." *We're gonna need another straw*. 24 October 2009. Web.

"When God Doesn't"

page 161 – Hutzler, Thomas. Qtd in Introduction, *Nurturing the Leader Within Your Child: What Every Parent Needs to Know*. By Tim Elmore. Nashville: Thomas Nelson Publishing, 2001. xi. Print.

page 163 – Job 23:1-5, paraphrase.

page 163 – Zacharias, Ravi. *Cries of the Heart: Bringing God Near When He Feels So Far*. Nashville: Word Publishing, 1998. 64. Print.

page 163 – Habakkuk 1:3a, New International Version, 1984.

page 163 – Psalm 10:1, New International Version, 2011.

page 163 – Jeremiah 15:18a, New International Version, 2011.

page 163 – Job 7:20, New International Version, 2011.

page 164 – Matthew 27:46b, New International Version, 2011.

page 164 – Yancey, Philip. *Disappointment with God*. Grand Rapids, MI: Zondervan, 1997. 253. Print.

page 166 – John 16:33b, New International Version, 2011.

page 166 – Galatians 1:4, New International Version, 2011.

page 166 – Romans 8:28, New International Version, 2011.

page 167 – Hebrews 11:32-35, New International Version, 2011.

page 167 – Hebrews 11:35-38, New International Version, 2011.

page 168 – Hebrews 11: 39a, New International Version, 2011.

page 170 – Hebrews 13:5b, New International Version, 2011.

page 170 – Hebrews 13:6a, New International Version, 2011.

page 170 – Romans 8:31, New International Version, 2011.

page 170 – Romans 8:32, New Living Translation.

page 171 – James 4:8a, New King James Version.

page 171 – Psalm 55:22a, New International Version, 2011.

page 172 – Isaiah 41:10, New International Version, 2011.

page 172 – 1 Corinthians 2:9, New International Version, 1984.

page 173 – John 6:66, New International Version, 2011.

page 174 – John 6:67, paraphrase.

page 174 – John 6:68-69, New International Version, 1984.

"Afterword"

page 176 - Niequist, Shauna. *Bittersweet: Thoughts on Change, Grace, and Learning the Hard Way*. Grand Rapids, MI: Zondervan, 2010. 238. Print.

page 176 – Niequist, Shauna. *Bittersweet: Thoughts on Change, Grace, and Learning the Hard Way*. Grand Rapids, MI: Zondervan, 2010. 241. Print.

page 176 – Niequist, Shauna. *Bittersweet: Thoughts on Change, Grace, and Learning the Hard Way*. Grand Rapids, MI: Zondervan, 2010. 240. Print.

page 177 – Ephesians 3:20, New International Version, 2011.